IMAGES OF
WORLD WAR II

IMAGES OF WORLD WAR II

Compiled by Rupert Matthews

Photographs supplied by Popperfoto

The Breedon Books
Publishing Company
Derby

First published in Great Britain by
The Breedon Books Publishing Company Limited
Breedon House, 44 Friar Gate, Derby, DE1 1DA.
1997

Photographs supplied by Popperfoto
Compiled by Rupert Matthews

ISBN 1 85983 072 2

Printed and bound by Butler & Tanner Ltd., Selwood Printing
Works, Caxton Road, Frome, Somerset.

Colour separations by Colour Services, Wigston, Leicester.

Jackets printed by Lawrence-Allen, Weston-super-Mare, Avon.

Contents

The Road to War

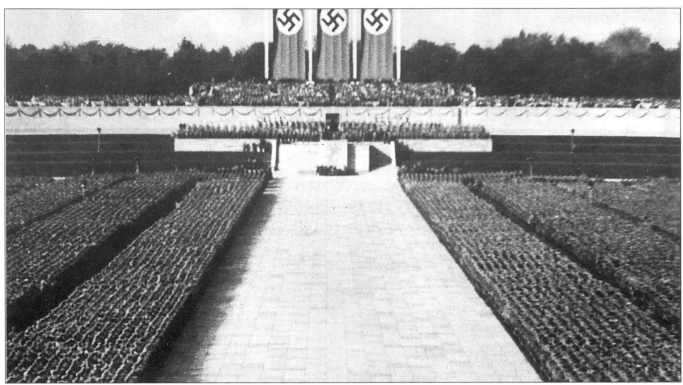

A Nazi Party rally at Nuremburg 1938. The rise of dictatorships in Germany, Italy, Spain and Japan seriously destabilised international relations during the 1930s. By stifling opposition at home and encouraging unquestioning obedience, the dictatorships ensured themselves absolute power. Other nations could only stand by and fear for what the future might bring.

The diplomatic corps of Europe meet at Versailles in 1919 to redraw the map of Europe. It was hoped the proceedings at Versailles would repeat the success of the 1815 Conference of Vienna after the Napoleonic Wars which ensured almost 100 years of peace. In fact, Versailles was a disaster which led to another world war only 20 years later.

US President Woodrow Wilson leads French Prime Minister Georges Clemenceau (right) and British Foreign Secretary Arthur Balfour (left) to the Versailles Conference. Clemenceau insisted on vindictive measures against Germany while Wilson demanded independence for the many small nations of eastern Europe. Balfour supported the other two in forming the League of Nations. None lived long enough to see their schemes fail.

A Nazi poster of February 1925 announces a speech by Adolf Hitler. The meeting was held shortly after his release from prison for staging an abortive coup in Bavaria. During his speech on Germany's future, Hitler denounced the Versailles Treaty as a betrayal of the German people. He blamed the Jews and international financiers, gaining much support for himself among the working classes.

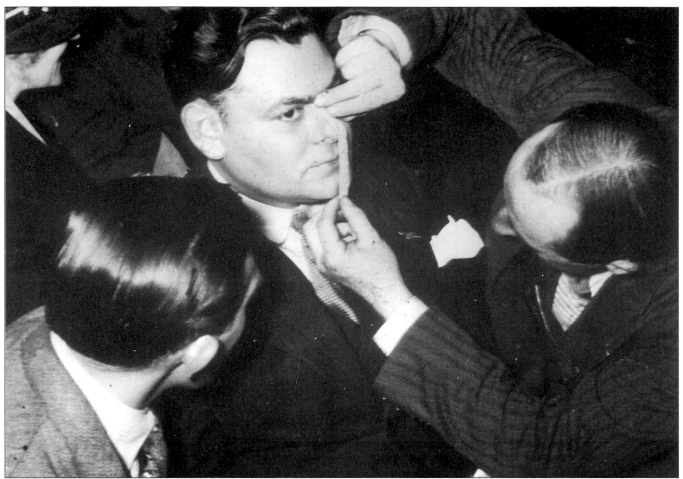

Nazi Government officials measure a man's nose to determine his Jewish ancestry. Once established in power after the general election of spring 1934, the Nazis passed a series of Enabling Acts which gave Hitler dictatorial powers. Persecution of the Jews was high on Hitler's list of priorities.

A midnight procession of Nazi student clubs in Saarbrucken in 1935. One of the Nazis most popular policies was that of uniting the German peoples into a 'Greater Germany'. A League of Nations plebiscite in 1935 returned the Saar to Germany, a crucial early victory for Hitler's foreign policy.

Physical training in youth camps, Germany 1935. Forbidden by the Versailles Treaty to have an army of more than 100,000 men, Germany turned to youth organisations to teach military skills such as sword drill, rifle firing and endurance marching.

A training exercise of the League of German Maidens at the 1936 Olympic Games in Berlin. While young German men were taught military skills, young women were encouraged to attain physical fitness and learn traditional home-making skills. The aim was produce a new generation of Aryan Germans fit to rule Europe.

A Chinese girl soldier guards a sandbag roadblock north of Shanghai, August 1937. While the dictators of Europe armed, the Japanese militarists had begun their career of conquest. In August 1937, some 200,000 Japanese troops attacked the great Chinese city of Shanghai, which held out until 8 November.

Chinese civilians flee the city of Chengtu after Japanese bombing. Having captured Manchuria, Shanghai and Peking by the close of 1937, the Japanese army threw itself into the conquest of China in 1938. Within three years the most prosperous regions of northern China had fallen to Japanese control.

Elite Italian Alpine troops at Massawa in Eritrea, 27 August 1935. Italy was the first of the European dictatorships to embark on a war of conquest when Mussolini ordered the invasion of Abyssinnia, one of the few African states not to become a European colony in the 19th century.

Abyssinian irregulars charge to attack an Italian outpost, probably near the Somali border. Although numerous and of legendary bravery, the Abyssinian tribesmen proved to be no match for the modern bombers and poison gas used by the Italians. The conquest of Abyssinnia was completed by 1936 and Emperor Haile Selassie fled to exile in Britain.

The declaration of a republic in Spain, 1931. The abdication of King Alfonso XIII left Spain leaderless and divided. Landowners, industrialists and fascists were ranged against regional separatists, socialists, commun ists and anarchists. In February 1936 a left-wing coalition won the general election and embarked on a programme of socialism. Army officers José Sanjurjo and Francisco Franco led a rebellion which plunged Spain into civil war.

Separated from her parents, a Basque child awaits her fate after Franco's troops capture Bilbao in 1937. The plight of refugees and the homeless would become a depressingly familiar sight as war engulfed first Spain and later all of Europe.

A makeshift armoured car captured by Franco's forces at Oviedo is displayed in the public square. Much of the fighting in Spain was between irregular troops who were poorly armed. Improvised weapons, such as this, were frequent features of the war, as were indiscipline and atrocities.

Italian troops parade in Rome after their return from fighting in Spain, 1938. Having failed to achieve a swift victory, General Franco called on his fellow fascists in Germany and Italy for help. Both Hitler and Mussolini

seized the chance to test new weapons and tactics. About
10,000 Germans and 50,0000 Italians fought in Spain.

The women of Tarragona pray for mercy from General Franco. After victory at the Battle of Ebro in November 1938, Franco's forces swept through Spain. On 25 January 1939 they captured Tarragona and then took Barcelona. Madrid fell a few days later and Franco was installed as the new head of a fascist dictatorship state.

German troops march across the Hohenzollern Bridge to reoccupy Cologne and the Rhineland in March 1936. Under the Versailles Treaty the area of Germany west of the Rhine, the Rhineland, was demilitarised. Hitler marched his men in to test the will of France and Britain. Their ineffective opposition convinced him that they were not seriously committed to the Treaty and encouraged his later conquests.

A display of German armed might during the Nazi rally at Nuremburg on 14 September 1937. Although banned by the Versailles Treaty from having tanks, the German army had developed their panzers in great secrecy. By 1937 Hitler was confident enough to flaunt his breaking of the Treaty in public.

A German band leads the Wehrmacht into Austria at Waldaassen on 3 October 1938. After years of economic crisis, murderous coups and virtual civil war, Austria was in no position to resist German annexation. Many Austrians welcomed the arrival of the Germans as a sign of stability and the return of peace and prosperity.

A trooper of the Czech cavalry watches intently as his political masters discuss the future of his nation. In September 1938 Britain and France agreed to German occupation of the Sudetenland. In March 1939 the Slovaks declared themselves independent and Germany occupied the Czech lands. The fate of Czechoslovakia convinced many in the West that Germany could only be stopped by the threat of war. Britain and France hurriedly formed alliances with Poland, next on the German list of conquests.

Phoney War

French troops guard a road near the front line, 11 December 1939. War finally broke out in Europe when Germany invaded Poland on 1 September 1939. After the swift Polish campaign, Europe settled down for the winter and what became known as the Phoney War. Apart from naval action and a few air skirmishes, there was almost no fighting. Troops on both sides became bored as they waited for the real action to begin.

The map of Poland signed by German foreign minister Joachim von Ribbentrop and Soviet dictator Stalin in August 1939. Although kept secret at the time, this marked the agreement between Hitler and Stalin which carved up eastern Europe between Germany and the Soviet Union, opening the way to the invasion of Poland.

Regular Polish infantry parade before marching to meet the invading Germans on 2 September 1939. On the outbreak of war, Poland was able to field 40 divisions. Against them Germany had 48 divisions available, the remaining 40 German divisions were stationed on the French frontier to guard against a French attack. With such odds, the Poles were confident of at least holding the German attack, and some Polish officers thought victory was assured.

Polish tanks mobilise for action. In 1939 Poland had one fully motorised brigade to support her infantry. However, the tanks were designed for close infantry support under cover of heavy field artillery rather than for independent action. Polish army officers had inherited their tactics from the Hapsburg Empire and had changed them little since victory over Russia in 1920.

A regiment of Polish lancers, supported by horse artillery, moves forward. Although much derided after 1939, the Poles had reasons to be confident of cavalry success. Much of Poland was marshy and the roads unsurfaced.

One heavy downpour would render the roads impassable to tanks or trucks and leave the fighting to cavalry and infantry which could move. But in September 1939 it did not rain.

A Warsaw shop is closed down and its owner thrown into prison after being convicted of black marketeering. On the declaration of war, Poland put long-prepared plans into action. Supplies of food and other necessities were controlled, and the 2.5 million reservists called up for military service.

Warsaw children watch German bombers pass overhead on 14 September. By this date the bulk of the Polish army was cut off from supplies and bases by the Germans on the west bank of the Vistula. The German Luftwaffe was sending its bombers on more long-range missions against cities and concentrations of Polish reserve troops.

Women and children dig trenches in Warsaw as the Germans advance. The blitzkrieg tactics of combined air, armoured and artillery assault took the Poles by surprise. By 8 September the Poles had fallen back 75 miles. That same day an advanced German armoured unit reached the outskirts of Warsaw, but was thrown back.

Sheltering behind a light panzer, German troops advance into the outskirts of Warsaw, 25 September. On 17 September the Soviet army invaded Poland from the east, sealing the fate of Poland. The high command and some 80,000 troops fled to neutral countries but several units were isolated and unable to escape. The Warsaw garrison was the largest, holding out until 28 September.

A Wehrmacht surveyor marks a post on the demarcation line between German and Soviet zones of occupied Poland. With the fighting at an end, the occupying powers established their rule. The Soviets murdered 15,000 captured Polish officers and sent all potential opponents to concentration camps. The German SS also rounded up political trouble makers and forced the Jews into ghettos.

An underground supply train in the Maginot Line. Begun in 1929, the Maginot Line was a series of interconnecting fortresses along France's eastern border. The deep bunkers armed with machine guns and artillery were designed to be impregnable. However, French military strategists were still thinking in terms of static trench warfare. Weaponry and mobile tactics had moved on and left the Maginot strategy behind.

French troops reinforce a trench with wooden fencing against winter rains. Two days after Germany invaded Poland, France and the British Empire declared war on Germany. As the Polish army was being overrun, the French began their mobilisation. The French army was not ready for battle until 17 September, by which time it was clear Poland was finished. The French army settled down to a defensive posture.

French soldiers put on amateur dramatics on Christmas Day 1939 in an underground storeroom of the Maginot Line. The Germans had originally scheduled their attack to begin on 12 November. However, bad weather set in and made panzer movements impossible. The attack was postponed until after Christmas.

A French despatch runner in the Vosges, January 1940. Gas was a real fear for both armies during the winter of 1940. Gas attacks had proved to be an effective and extremely unpleasant weapon during the trench warfare of World War One. All soldiers were required to carry gas masks and perform regular drills. In the event, gas proved unsuitable in mobile warfare and it was never used.

French soldiers clear snow from a village street in the Vosges, January 1940. During a blizzard on 10 January an aircraft carrying a German staff officer with the entire German battle plans became lost and landed in Belgium. The Germans realised their strategy was now revealed and began drawing up fresh plans. The attack was postponed yet again.

French airmen inspect a propaganda leaflet before a February 1940 mission to drop thousands on the German army. Allied commanders believed that propaganda leaflets might disrupt morale in the German army. In fact the ordinary German soldier was supremely confident after the easy victory in Poland. It was the senior officers who were apprehensive of attacking France.

French and British airmen inspect models of German aircraft and discuss air tactics. During the phoney war, air activity was limited to patrols and reconnaissance flights. When the German assault began in earnest, the pre-war fliers quickly learnt their carefully practised tactics were unsuited to combat flying and reverted to techniques used in World War One.

German troops play cards in a rear area of the Western Front, March 1940. German generals were by this time seriously concerned about the morale of their men. The assault had been postponed three times and many units had been moved from billet to billet as the plans changed and developed over the winter.

French troops return to barracks after helping local farmers, March 1940. Officers had to use all their ingenuity to keep the men busy and try to raise morale during the seven months of waiting in the Phoney War.

Marshal Gamelin suggested marching into Belgium to threaten the Ruhr, but he was overruled by politicians anxious to avoid invading a neutral country.

French artillery men in a concealed emplacement near the Belgian border. The Maginot Line had not been constructed along the Belgian border for financial and

diplomatic reasons. As a result defences on this stretch of land were weak. The bulk of the French and British field armies were stationed here to meet any attack.

A French infantry man checks his rat for signs of gas. Along the border the French had erected a string of such rat boxes on posts as it was widely assumed that a German attack would be preceded by the use of gas. Regular checking of the rats was a detested duty in the front line.

The long wait of the Phoney War is over. The men of this battery of French horse artillery move north towards the Aisne and an uncertain future as German troops pour over the border on their blitzkrieg offensive.

German army cooks distribute supplementary rations of eggs and cheese, April 1940. The morale of the troops was vital as the date of the assault drew nearer and German generals took great pains to ensure their troops were fit and in good spirits.

A French anti-aircraft battery complete with aircraft detector. Lacking effective radar, the French relied upon these giant earphones to detect aircraft engines while the machines themselves were still out of sight or above cloud. Skilled operators could estimate aircraft numbers, height and heading with surprising accuracy.

Blitzkrieg

German troops march unopposed into a Danish town. On 9 April 1940, the Germans invaded Denmark and overran the small country by mid-morning. Only one Danish aircraft managed to take off, but it was shot down almost at once. In all 13 Danes were killed before King Christian ordered a surrender. The German censor has painted out the sign on the left-hand shop to disguise the exact location of this photograph.

The burning of Elvarum, Norway. German forces invaded Norway without warning on 9 April 1940. After initial confusion, the Norwegian armed forces put up fierce resistance to the invasion. The town of Elvarum was bombed by the Luftwaffe on 4 May and set alight. Almost the entire town was destroyed by fire, and 30 civilians lost their lives. Norway surrendered on 10 June.

A wrecked German glider on a captured airfield. The German assault in the West opened on 10 May. It was heralded by a new and terrifying weapon, glider troops. Descending from the dawn skies, a force of just 500 men captured the bridges over the Albert Canal and destroyed the supposedly impregnable Belgian fortress of Eben Emael with demolition charges. The route into Belgium was open.

German panzers rumble through Malmedy just days after the attack began. Malmedy had formerly been part of Germany, but had been given to Belgium by the Versailles Treaty. Its reincorporation into Germany was a benefit of the thrust into Belgium.

Jubilant German-speaking Alsations welcome the Wehrmacht on their release from a French internment camp, June 1940. The border province of Alsace had been given to France in 1919, but large numbers of the population were ethnic Germans. These people were rounded up and imprisoned by the French when war broke out.

A German light tank pushes through a forest on the way into France. The new plan for the invasion of France was developed by Erich von Manstein. It called for independent columns of armour to storm through the Ardennes and then plunge deep behind Allied lines. The armour was to be led by Heinz Guderian, nickname 'Hurry Heinz' for his belief in mobile warfare.

German infantry use dinghies to cross a river. Manstein's plan depended on getting across the Meuse on the fourth day of the assault, then speeding ahead behind the main Allied forces. The French had blown the bridges at Sedan as expected. While Stuka dive-bombers and artillery pounded the defences, infantry paddled across in dinghies and secured a bridgehead.

German engineers finish erecting a wooden bridge, May 1940. The German infantry crossed the Meuse at Sedan at 4pm on 13 May. Engineers at once began work on a temporary bridge, even though they were constructing it under fire. The bridge was completed by midnight and an entire panzer division was across by dawn. By 5pm Guderian had his whole force over the Meuse and he began the drive west.

Luftwaffe chief Hermann Goering listens while Wehrmacht officers explain the advance to him, May 1940. By 16 May, Guderian had advanced 50 miles beyond the Meuse and faced no serious opposition. The High Command kept track of Guderian's movements as he swept behind the Allied armies, and ordered panzer divisions further north to co-operate.

View from a German bomber as it swoops down on a retreating French column, 1940. The Luftwaffe was used to destroy battlefield targets in co-operation with ground forces, but also had the task of spreading destruction and mayhem far behind the lines. The bombing and strafing of roads miles from the fighting became commonplace across northern France.

German cavalry advance across France, 1940. Although often thought of as a motorised army, the Wehrmacht of 1940 included many cavalry units. Their main task was to advance behind the panzers to sweep up Allied stragglers. The advancing infantry, far behind would deal with any sizeable garrisons of the enemy. his photograph was taken by General Erwin Rommel, a cavalry officer who by this time commanded the 7th Panzer Division.

A German propaganda picture with the caption, 'Trenches don't stop the advance of our infantry'. Although trenches were made obsolete by Guderian's panzer tactics, propaganda chief Josef Goebbels believed the German public needed images of German soldiers overcoming the obstacles which had hindered them in World War One.

German engineers at work on a landing stage on the Belgian coast. The Belgians had long expected to be invaded and had laid demolition charges on all major bridges and other structures which might be of use to the invader. German engineers were kept busy repairing the damage done by the retreating Belgians.

German infantry storm a railway station in northern France. The swift capture of intact rail lines was to prove vital for the later stages of the German advance when supplies had to be moved in great quantity for many miles.

Wehrmacht bicycle troops dive for cover as Allied troops open fire. Many infantry battalions had bicycle troops for use as detached reconnaissance units or for carrying messages if the fragile field radios became damaged.

A pigeon carrier attached to a German infantry unit during the invasion of France. Battlefield communication was vital to German plans for mobile warfare. Homing pigeons were used to carry reports from advancing units back to headquarters to keep the general staff up to date on troop movements and enemy activity.

A column of infantry and horse-drawn transport moves through a village in northern France. The men are not wearing helmets, and clearly expect no immediate trouble. Many advancing infantry units found they had no enemies to fight as the French and British had been swept away by the panzers and motorised infantry.

The ruins of a Dutch frontier fortress after being pounded by Stuka dive-bombers and German artillery. Those fortresses not on the immediate route of advance were bypassed and isolated by the Germans, to be dealt with later by reserve troops.

German infantry rest on the pavement of a French town, eating biscuits and cakes bought from a local shop. At this stage in the war German officers were generally scrupulous in paying for goods requisitioned from civilians as they had no wish to alienate the local population in what many expected to be a swift victory and short occupation.

A German war correspondent types his report on the seat of a panzer command car near Boulogne. Goebbels insisted that reporters accompany the front line units together with cameramen to produce dramatic reports for his propaganda ministry to feed to the German people.

A panzer advances through farmland on its route to the Channel. Contrary to popular belief, the German panzers were smaller and less heavily armoured than their French opponents, and available in smaller numbers. It was their organisation into armoured divisions with motorised infantry and the leadership of men such as Guderian which made the panzers so formidable in combat.

The beach outside Dunkirk as the British troops wait to be taken off by small boats and the Royal Navy. General Gort had realised his army might be cut off as early as 16 May, but did not order a retreat to Dunkirk until ten days later. Next day, 27 May, the Belgian army surrendered and the British retreat became a race to reach Dunkirk before the German panzers.

Survivors climb aboard a naval ship off Dunkirk during the evacuation. Operation Dynamo, to rescue the trapped British army from France, began on 26 May. Four days later the main British army reached Dunkirk and established a firm defensive box against German attacks. Luftwaffe bombing raids became increasingly frequent and by 2 June daylight evacuations had to be abandoned.

Some of the small private yachts return to the Thames above Oxford after helping bring back troops from Dunkirk. Hundreds of small craft made the perilous Channel crossing and braved German attacks to help save the troops. Many were manned by the navy, but others were crewed by their owners. Over 100 were lost during the operation.

Cigarettes and fruit are handed to Dunkirk survivors as their train arrives in London, 31 May. In all 224,000 British and over 100,000 French and Belgian troops were rescued from Dunkirk between 26 May and 4 June. The cost had been high, with six destroyers, eight transport ships and 200 other craft lost off Dunkirk.

Some of the tanks, vehicles and other heavy equipment abandoned by the British and French around Dunkirk. Stripped of their equipment, the British troops who escaped were in no state to fight again and Britain would have been virtually defenceless if German troops had landed.

A German tank crew proudly display the painting on their tank turret which commemorates their sinking of a British warship in the fighting around Dunkirk. Having eliminated the Dunkirk pocket, the Germans turned south towards Paris.

French tanks moving to block the German advance on Paris in June 1940. After the stunning German victories in northern France, Marshal Weygrand was left with 47 French and two British divisions. The Germans had ten panzer and 130 infantry divisions. For several days the fighting was fiercer than any yet seen, but the French defence line on the Somme collapsed on 9 June.

A Paris schoolroom strewn with debris from a German bomb blast. The German advance crossed the Marne on 11 June and swept into Paris three days later. The French government had already fled to Tours and Marshall Weygrand was ordered to form a defensive line on the Loire.

Originally captioned 'Collecting scrap for German foundries' this German propaganda photograph shows German soldiers inspecting captured French equipment abandoned by retreating forces. By 16 June, the French armies had collapsed into a mass of fleeing men hardly keeping to their units.

A German Luftwaffe officer adds a new badge to his walking stick. He has adapted the habit of adding badges depicting places visited by inscribing the names of battles in which he fought during the conquest of France which, in less than two months of fighting, was considered a great victory and seemed to vindicate Hitler's policies.

The signing of the Franco-German armistace on 22 June. On 16 June, Marshall Weygrand informed the French government that he was defeated and advised surrender. The government sent a message to Hitler asking for terms. Hitler wanted to impose humiliation. He arranged for the armistace to be signed in the same railway coach in the Forest of Compiegne where the German armies had surrendred in 1918.

German officers prepare to fly the flag of Guernsey to Berlin as a war trophy. The invasion of the Channel Islands followed swiftly after the collapse of France. Lying close to the French coast and almost undefended, the islands proved to be any easy target for German troops. Thus, part of Britain came under occupation.

A German army officer discusses occupation regulations with a policeman on Jersey, September 1940. As the only part of the British Isles to suffer German occupation, the Channel Islands had to cope with unaccustomed foreign rule. Men of military age had largely been evacuated, leaving women, old men and children who attempted to lead as normal a life as possible.

In the autumn of 1940 the loyal Channel islanders began a campaign of painting swastikas on the houses of collaborators. In response, the German army daubed swastikas on every house in the affected area.

German officers proudly show the vanquished Maginot Line to visiting Japanese officers. In an ominous move for the future, German and Japanese dictators began sharing military and diplomatic secrets as the hostility of the United States to them both became clearer.

The Blitz

After the fall of France, Britain stood alone against the might of Nazi Germany. Hitler hoped Britain would agree to a peace and even ordered the demobilisation of 35 reserve divisions. When it became clear Britain would not surrender, Hitler threw the might of German air power at Britain first in what became known as the Battle of Britain and then the Blitz.

Clearing up after a German bombing attack on Orkney, 15 March 1940. Although the German air offensive against Britain is generally reckoned to have begun in July 1940, attacks had been carried out earlier. The first civilian casualty was Jim Isbister, killed during this raid on the Orkneys by German bombers operating from Norway.

German mechanics at work on a Dornier 88 medium bomber. The Luftwaffe began the air campaign against Britain with a formidable force of 998 bombers, 316 dive-bombers and 929 fighters. However, the men were trained in Blitzkrieg tactics of close co-operation with ground forces and had little idea of how to wage an all-air conflict without ground support.

German bomber pilots identify their target before taking off for a raid on southern England. The initial aim of the Luftwaffe attacks was to destroy the RAF and so secure control of the air. Only then could the German navy safely escort the army to the beaches at Folkestone and Brighton where they intended to land.

A squadron of Messerschmitt 109 fighter aircraft drawn up on an airfield in northern France, summer 1940. The main fighter aircraft available to the Luftwaffe for the assault on Britain, the 109 was a top class fighting aircraft, but lacked endurance. The task of escorting bombers badly stretched the aircraft's flying time.

Sir Trafford Leigh-Mallory, Air Chief Marshal Lord Dowding and General Pile (left to right). Dowding, a veteran of air fighting during World War One, commanded RAF Fighter Command during the Battle of Britain. Leigh-Mallory, another World War One air veteran, commanded the fighter groups which faced the brunt of the Luftwaffe assault. Pile commanded the anti-aircraft batteries.

RAF fighter pilots attend a lecture on German aircraft and air tactics between missions. Many of the British pilots during the Battle of Britain were young and inexperienced in combat flying. They needed as much advice on German tactics and capabilities as they could get.

Scramble! RAF pilots run to their Hurricane fighter aircraft 'somewhere in southern England'. Although often given advance warning of German attacks by the Observer Corps and radar, British pilots had to be on immediate standby to tackle the massed waves of Luftwaffe forces.

Spitfires of an Australian squadron take off to face an incoming raid. The pilots fighting to defend Britain came from many nations. Not only did the Empire and Commonwealth contribute men, but survivors of the Polish, French and Czech air forces either flew with the RAF or formed their own squadrons. The Poles, in particular, were highly regarded by the British.

Hop-pickers in Kent nervously watch the aerial battle over head. Although RAF bases near the southern coast were the main target of German bombers during August, the pilots were likely to drop their bombs almost anywhere if hard pressed by RAF fighters and civilian casualties rose alarmingly.

A civilian couple watch the vapour trails of dog-fighting aircraft high over Surrey. This was all that most British civilians saw of the Battle of Britain which was fought mainly at high altitude during the long, glorious summer of 1940.

A Stuka dive-bomber, its undercarriage shot away by RAF fighters, limps home towards northern France. The Stuka had proved itself an invaluable weapon during the invasion of France, providing extremely accurate bombing support to ground troops. However, it was vulnerable to enemy fighters and on 18 August the Luftwaffe withdrew it from the Battle of Britain.

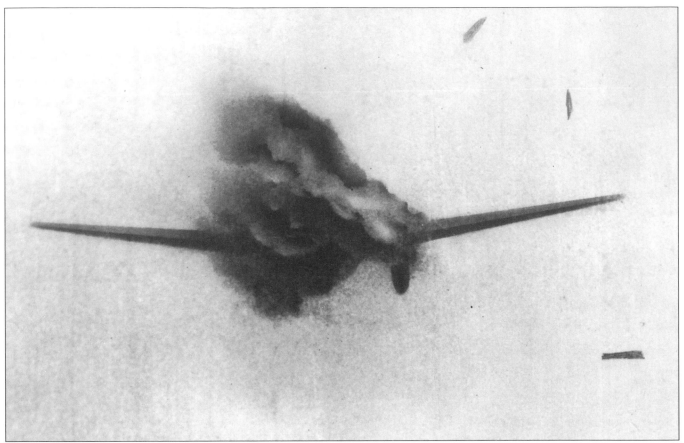

Smoke engulfs a Heinkel III bomber as seen from the Hurricane fighter which attacked it. Hurricanes and Spitfires were each equipped with eight machine guns. Pilots, however, often complained that their weapons had little effect on German bombers and the machine guns were later replaced with 20mm cannon.

Hurricanes return to base at dusk, watched by anxious ground crew who look for casualties. By early September the RAF was losing 120 pilots a week, with only 65 arriving from training. With pilots flying combat missions almost all day, tiredness and increasing nervous irritation became major problems.

RAF ground crew work on a Spitfire while another circles overhead. In September the Luftwaffe switched strategy from attacking RAF bases to bombing cities. The change gave hard pressed ground crew the chance to repair battered aircraft and put up more effective resistance to the bombers.

The plotting room of Anti-Aircraft Control Headquarters, London. The ATS girls plot incoming bombers while the officers issue telephone instructions to batteries regarding height and direction of enemy aircraft. During this period, anti-aircraft guns were relatively ineffective at inflicting damage, but did force pilots to fly at high altitude, making their bombing less accurate.

St Paul's Cathedral seen through the shattered ruins of St Mary-le-Bow. On 7 September the Luftwaffe began its massed raids on London. The destruction of St Mary-le-Bow symbolised the devastation visited on London's East End during the Blitz, as a true cockney was, by tradition, born within the sound of Bow Bells.

Firemen, their backs to St Paul's Cathedral, fight the flames engulfing the offices and shops beside the cathedral. Although the area around the cathedral was almost entirely destroyed, the church remained and was regarded as a symbol of London's defiance.

London firemen try in vain to save St Bride's Church, a masterpiece of Restoration architecture by Sir Christopher Wren. After Hitler postponed invasion plans on 12 October, the Luftwaffe assault on London intensified. Incendiaries and high explosives were rained down in an attempt to bomb the city into submission.

Bomb damage at the House of Commons, December 1940. By December, the Germans had 750 bombers available for night attacks on British cities, each able to carry over three tons of bombs. London was attacked for 57 consecutive nights by 160 bombers, while smaller forces attacked provincial cities.

Auxiliary firemen drink a cup of tea provided by a café in central London which they have just saved by putting out a fire caused by an incendiary bomb in an adjoining building, 30 September 1940 The fire services proved to be the salvation of London as incendiaries were used in an attempt to start a 'second great fire of London'.

Mobile canteens provided by American volunteers serve food to the bombed-out homeless in Coventry. By the severe winter of 1940-41 public opinion in America had swung decisively behind Britain, although actual participation in the war was opposed. War equipment was provided by the American government and numerous volunteer and fund-raising organisations sprang up to help the people of Britain.

Their office made unsafe by high explosives, an accounts department staff continue work in a side street, London, 17 October 1940. Despite the widespread damage caused by bombing, civilians attempted to carry on with their normal lives. For many, business as usual became a matter of pride and defiance to the Nazi bombers.

A London shop keeper makes a virtue of a necessity after his shop was bombed on 17 October 1940. Blast damaged clothes and models are put on display in the shop window to attract the attention of passers-by.

A wrecked terrace street in Liverpool. The docks of Liverpool handled a large proportion of Britain's imports of food and war equipment and so were a prime target for German bombers. However, the city was near the limit of the range of aircraft operating from France. Bombing was inaccurate and large areas of the city were damaged.

The ruins of Coventry Cathedral after the great raid of 14 November 1940. Code-named Moonlight Sonata, the Luftwaffe raid was designed to be a showpiece operation. New navigation aids were used to target a pathfinder force on to the city centre on a night of brilliant moonlight. Every German aircraft available was put into the air. The city centre was obliterated and there were enormous numbers of casualties.

Blast damage being repaired in Dover. Bombing was not the only weapon the German could employ against Britain. Dover and nearby towns came under regular bombardment by long-range artillery based around Calais during the late summer and autumn of 1940. The RAF flew bombing raids to silence the guns.

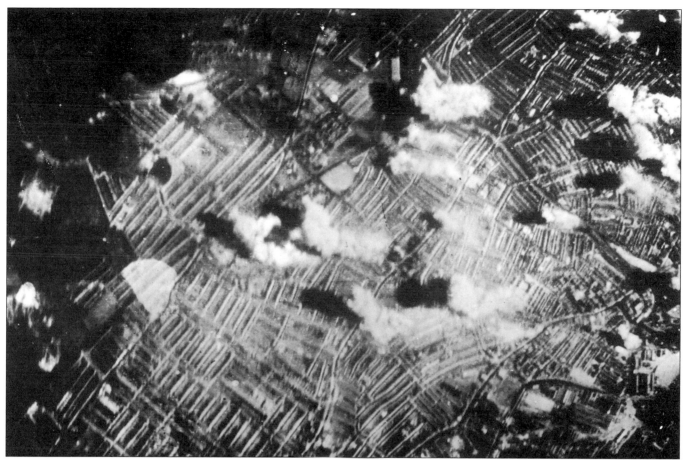

View from a German bomber of a raid on Southampton in 1941. As a major port, Southampton was a prime target for Germany in its campaign to aid the U-boats in disrupting food imports and so starve Britain into surrender.

Bomb damage at Exeter Cathedral, 5 December 1940. By December the Luftwaffe was bombing almost every town and city of any size. The decision to ease pressure on the major industrial cities was a relief to British officials trying to organise production of arms and war equipment.

The fire-gutted ruins of the Guildhall, York, destroyed by a raid in April 1941. Bad weather had kept the Luftwaffe away from more distant targets such as York during January and February and most of March, but the bombing raids returned in strength as the spring weather improved.

Workers search the wreckage of a street in Bath, levelled by a massive air mine in April 1941. The censor did not release this photograph until 26 May. During the Blitz a policy was followed of holding back photographs and reports until at least 28 days after a raid, and even then not until a second raid on the same target had taken place. It was known that German intelligence read British newspapers in neutral countries and it was hoped this policy would cause confusion.

After a lull in heavy attacks during the winter, a new 'mini-blitz' was launched in April. Birmingham was subjected to two consecutive nights of heavy bombing on 12 and 13 April. The raids proved to be the end of the all-out offensive as the bulk of Luftwaffe forces were shifted east in May to prepare for-the invasion of Russia.

Central Plymouth after the bombing raids which tore the heart from the city. One of the most badly damaged cities in Britain during the war, Plymouth faced a massive rebuilding task when peace was restored.

Maids peer though a window in Norwich, April 1943. Even after the main Blitz ended in the spring of 1941, German bombers continued to raid towns and cities of Britain on occasion, inflicting much damage and many casualties.

War in Russia

The German invasion of the Soviet Union in the summer of 1941 began well for the Nazis. All major objectives were captured on time and vast Soviet armies were destroyed in weeks. But the coming of winter led to a stalemate which ultimately proved fatal to Hitler's plans The barbaric treatment of civilians by the Nazis behind the lines led the Soviets to embark on a war of revenge which would not finish until Germany lay prostrate and devastated.

Soviet armoured cars parade in Moscow, September 1939. When German and Soviet forces met in Poland in 1939, the Germans were amazed by such obsolete equipment and the poor training and morale of the Soviet armies. Their reports convinced Hitler that the Soviet Union was so weak militarily that it could be conquered in only four months.

Romanian infantry parade through Bucharest, summer 1940. Romania had recently suffered from Soviet aggression and greatly feared Stalin's motives along the lower Danube. As a result, Romania eagerly joined the German plan to attack the Soviet Union, contributing seven full divisions and several detached brigades. Later Hungary, and many ethnic groups within the Soviet Union joined the German forces.

A German sleeps exhausted during the advance into the Soviet Union, July 1941. In the early weeks of the attack everything went well for the Germans. Hundreds of thousands of prisoners were captured, thousands of tanks and aircraft destroyed and the panzer columns were pushing deep into Soviet territory.

The Soviets were entirely unprepared for the German assault and were taken completely by surprise. In an effort to bolster civilian morale photographs of pre-war training exercises were issued This one, released on 23 June, was said to show Soviet paratroops landing behind German forces to cut their lines of support. No such attack took place.

A machine gun unit from a Kirghiz regiment of the Red Army. With almost the entire professional Red Army destroyed by November 1941, the Soviet Union turned to reservists and second-line forces. There was a general mobilisation of men and a movement of forces to the west.

A German mobile kitchen struggles through a ford in Russia, autumn 1941. When the autumn rains came, the fundamental weakness of the German army was revealed. The bulk of supply and transport relied on wheels and became hopelessly bogged down. General Guderian wanted to launch a race for Moscow, but was over-ruled.

A few of the 600,000 Soviet troops captured at Kiev in September 1941. German military strategists had estimated the Soviets could mobilise 200 divisions, about 4 million men. By October the Germans had already

killed, captured or wounded 8.5 million Soviets, and still
were faced by over 100 divisions.

German troops in makeshift snow camouflage, December 1941. The onset of the Russian winter was disastrous for the German forces. Lacking proper snow camouflage they made easy targets and many resorted to torn sheets, as did these men. Others, lacking proper winter clothing, suffered from frostbite.

Soviet troops advance under fire, dragging a mortar on sleds. Well accustomed to the harsh Russian winter, the Soviets were equipped with warm clothing and such simple but effective equipment as the sleds shown here. The arrival of fresh elite units from Siberia in December 1941 saved Moscow from capture by the advancing Germans.

Germans surrender to the advancing Red Army near Vyasma, west of Moscow, April 1942. The Red Army advances of the winter came to a halt by May as their superiority in winter warfare was negated by the onset of spring.

A Crimean woman mourns the death of her son, shot along with other civilian hostages by the Germans at Kerch. The brutality of the Nazi occupation of Russia was appalling. Thousands were executed for trivial offences, while Jews were shot out of hand. Hundreds of thousands died in the first year of occupation as Nazi officials took over administration from the army.

Three Soviet pilots pose with their British Hurricane fighters in the summer of 1942. In the wake of the German onslaught, Soviet Russia was desperately short of modern equipment and Churchill agreed to send convoys through the Arctic Ocean to deliver supplies to the Soviets until their own factories could enter full production.

A pair of Red Navy men guard an observation post near Rostov. Driven from their main base at Sevastopol by the German advance, the ground forces of the Red Navy joined the Red Army in the desperate defence of the southern front against a renewed German offensive as summer allowed the panzers to move again.

A small Soviet Partisan unit inspects their maps before a raid on German supply lines. Given high priority in equipment and supply by Stalin, the Partisan units operated hundreds of miles behind German lines and achieved great success in disrupting the regular supply of arms and reinforcements from the autumn of 1942 onwards.

A Soviet tank squadron is given its orders before advancing to meet the Germans near Stalingrad in November 1942. The appearance of these T34 tanks some months earlier had been a nasty shock to the German panzer commanders. The sloping armour and powerful guns of the T34 made them superior to most German tanks.

A German Panzer IV hits a mine in the snow, December 1942. In November 1942, some 200,000 Germans were cut off in Stalingrad by a surprise Soviet offensive. Manstein launched a combined panzer and infantry assault to relieve the surrounded men, but his attack was driven back by 28 December.

German prisoners are paraded by the Red Army for propaganda pictures north of Stalingrad, December 1942. Goering had promised that his Luftwaffe could keep the surrounded troops supplied with food and ammunition, but it was a vain boast. His failure led to his disgrace and virtual retirement.

The shattered city of Stalingrad on 29 January 1943. Outnumbered by four to one and suffering lack of supplies the Germans in Stalingrad gradually collapsed under Soviet pressure. The last units surrendered or were exterminated on 2 February 1943. The Germans had lost nearly 300,000 men.

Soviet cavalry advancing in the Caucasus in January 1943. In the harsh mountain conditions cavalry were more mobile than motorised units and as effective as infantry. The Soviet advance from Stalingrad threatened to cut off German units in the Caucasus, causing their retreat by January 1943.

A column of German Panzer IVs move up to attempt to stop the Soviet attack at Orel, August 1943. A massive German armoured attack at Kursk failed in July with the loss of about 40 tanks per month. It was to be the last major German attack in the East and the high tide of the German campaign in the Soviet Union.

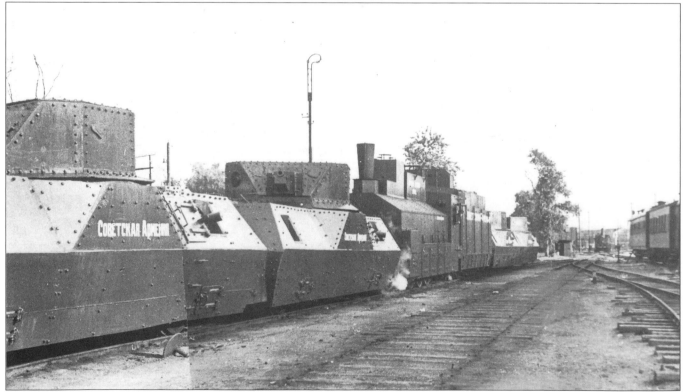

A Soviet armoured train awaits its load of supply trucks. By the late summer of 1943 it had become clear that the campaign in the Soviet Union would be decided by logistics as much as by fighting. Heavily armed and armoured engines such as this were essential to protect supply trains against aerial or guerrilla attacks.

Red Army infantry advance warily behind a T34 on the lower Don. After victory at Kursk and Orel in the summer of 1943, the Soviets went on the attack. Their strategy was to build up massive superiority of men and equipment and push ahead until German reinforcements halted the advance. meanwhile men and supplies would be stockpiled elsewhere for another attack. In this way the Germans were kept under pressure.

A Soviet ski patrol pushes through the forests north of the Black Sea. By the winter of 1943 German generals were urging a flexible strategy. They were confident their superior equipment and men could use swift movement and tactical initiative to hold against odds of six to one. They thought they could exhaust the Soviet Union into a compromise peace. Hitler refused, ordering a policy of no retreat from key positions.

German troops surrendering to Soviets on the Central Front. The Germans are handing in 'Surrender Passes' issued by the Soviets which promised good treatment to those troops not members of the SS or the Nazi Party. Hitler's orders of no retreat meant that many units were cut off and isolated, causing the men to surrender rather than die defending hopeless positions.

German engineers blow up a bridge over the Dune River in Latvia as they fall back before the Red Army, July 1944. By the summer of 1944 the German armies were in retreat before the Soviets. Over 200,000 troops were cut off by the Soviets in Latvia and held out until after the death of Hitler and surrender of Germany in May 1945.

Japanese Offense

Japanese troops march unopposed into Rangoon, 8 March 1942 The Japanese onslaught in East Asia surprised and shocked the Allies. Within a few months the Japanese Empire had conquered vast new territories, destroyed the armed forces of the Allies in the region and achieved a reputation for invincible bravery. But in the very success of the onrush they had made mistakes which would eventually lead to defeat.

A photograph taken of Japanese ambassador to Washington, Komura (right), with special envoy Kurusu, as they entered the State Department on 7 December 1941 to deliver the declaration of war. Komura anxiously checks the time as he is aware that his nation would be attacking that day and that the declaration had to be delivered first. In fact Japanese aircraft were already bombing Pearl Harbor.

The Japanese aircraft carrier *Kaga* in 1941 The Kaga was one of the main Japanese ships used to launch the strike at Pearl Harbor. Along with other major Japanese ships she left port on 26 November under the command of Admiral Ohuichi Nagumo, who observed strict radio silence. His orders were to attack the US Naval base at Pearl Harbor, unless ordered not to do so.

Japanese Zero fighters take off from an aircraft carrier to launch the attack on Pearl Harbor, 7 December 1941 The initial strike force was composed of 49 bombers, 51 dive-bombers, 51 fighters and 40 torpedo-bombers specially trained to cope with the shallow waters of Pearl Harbor.

A photograph taken by a bomber in the first attack wave on Pearl Harbor. The Americans were taken entirely by surprise, with most of their men on weekend leave. The only American aircraft in the air was a force of bombers arriving almost out of fuel. They were shot down instantly. Japanese losses were very light and occurred mainly among the second attack wave as anti-aircraft gunners reached their weapons.

The destroyer USS *Shaw* explodes as a bomb strikes her ammunition store during the attack on Pearl Harbor. Japanese dive-bombing was very accurate during the attack and accounted for much of the damage. Conventional bombers concentrated on shore targets, including air bases.

An American destroyer, forced ashore during the Japanese attack on Pearl Harbor, is inspected by repair teams. In all the US lost seven battleships, three destroyers and almost half the aircraft at the base. The US Navy in the Pacific was effectively destroyed as a fighting force, allowing the Japanese a free hand throughout the Pacific for their transport ships and invasion forces.

A Filipino air raid warden bows to a statue of Christ he has rescued from a church bombed by the Japanese. The Japanese assault on the Philippines began on 10 December. In less than a month the American and Filipino forces were under siege on the island of Corregidor and the Bataan Peninsula. They held out until 6 May.

The battleship USS *Pennsylvania* sits almost undamaged behind two smashed destroyers while dock facilities burn beyond just hours after the attack on Pearl Harbor. Although the fleet was devastated, the US shore facilities were only slightly damaged. In particular the oil refinery was untouched. Furthermore the US carriers were at sea on manoeuvre when the attack struck and escaped damage.

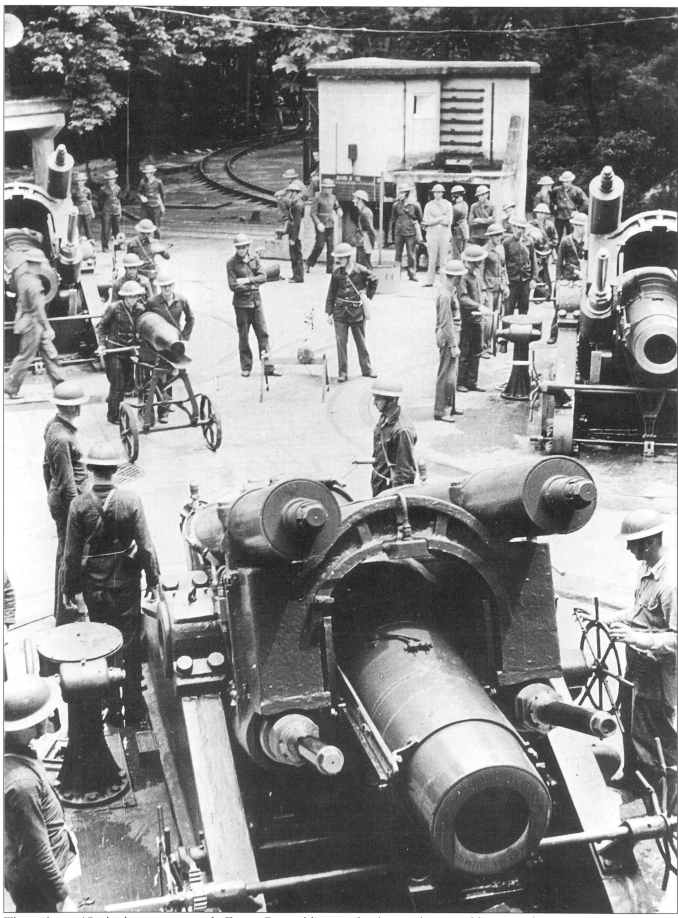

The giant 12 inch mortars of Fort Corregidor, Philippines, in the autumn of 1941. As apparently invulnerable as the fortresses of the French Maginot Line two years earlier, the defences of the Philippines were obsolete and manned by second rate troops. They would prove to be just as weak as other pre-war static defences when put to the test.

Scottish troops, supported by an armoured car, defend a road north of Singapore during a training exercise in November 1941. The British believed that the Malayan jungles were impenetrable to armed forces and concentrated on defending the roads. The strategy proved to be a costly mistake when the Japanese invaded.

The liner *Empress of Asia* burns off Singapore after attack by Japanese aircraft in 1942. The Japanese invasion of Malaya began on 8 December 1941 and by 31 January 1942 had driven the British south to the city-fortress of Singapore. A Japanese attack on 8 February led to desper-ate fighting but, cut off from fresh water and faced by Japanese threats of massacring the civilians, the British surrendered. It was the most humiliating defeat a British army ever suffered.

Japanese reinforcements land at Moulmein on the Salween River. The Japanese invasion of Burma began on 20 January 1942, with an assault on Moulmein. Just 35,000 men were sent to capture Burma, but the British had only two under-strength divisions in the country and could offer only a limited defence.

Japanese solders advance into Pegu, 4 March 1942. Pegu was a major road and rail junction which played a key role in British plans to defend Burma. Its capture ensured the collapse of British resistance in southern Burma and precipitated a retreat to Mandalay.

A Japanese soldier guards the docks at Rangoon. The capital of Burma was captured on 8 March after the British were forced to retreat by defeats elsewhere. The British and Burmese armies withdrew 400 miles north to form a defensive line around Mandalay.

Japanese bicycle troops push through the Burmese jungles. Japanese success at moving large numbers of men along poor jungle roads enabled them to manoeuvre with a speed and flexibility which took the British completely by surprise. On 26 April, the Japanese outflanked the 60,000 British and Imperial troops defending Mandalay, forcing them to fall back towards India.

British troops man a machine gun nest in the the densely forested hills on the Burma-India border. The Japanese advance finally halted on the border and both sides dug into defensive positions. Despite determined assaults by both sides, the front line remained fairly static until 1944.

A British Hurricane bomber being prepared for a mission on the Burma front. British forces had suffered badly from lack of air power during the initial Japanese onslaught and the development of effective air forces were a priority. Even so, the British army in India largely had to make do with equipment considered almost obsolete in the European theatre.

Under Occupation

Hitler in Paris with senior military and Nazi party figures. The fate of those subjected to German occupation varied greatly. In part treatment varied according to the senior army or Nazi official in the region. Elsewhere official policy varied between the wooing of occupied Aryans in Scandinavia and the merciless massacres carried out in Russia. Nazi occupations proved to be among the most brutal in history.

German horse artillery march into Paris past the Arc de Triomphe in June 1940. At this point most people expected Germany to win a swift victory over Britain and agree peace terms. As the occupation was expected to be relatively short both the Germans and French did little to antagonise the other and life assumed an uneasy feeling of near normality.

German troops pay their respects to the Tomb of the Unknown Warrior in Paris, probably in July 1940. Over 90,000 Frenchmen had died during the blitzkrieg defeat of their nation. Choosing to work through native French local government, the German army of occupation at first had little to do with ordinary French civilians.

A German officer browses at a second hand book stall during the early weeks of the German occupation of Paris. By September 1941 French resentment was targeted at the British. Not only had the Royal Navy sunk the French fleet at Mers-el-Khebir, but the RAF was bombing military targets in northern France, and accidentally killing French civilians.

German soldiers on a tram reserved for their use in Paris, May 1942. As the occupation became prolonged, the early tolerance vanished. In May 1941 the French police had been ordered to apprehend all foreign Jews and turn them over to the Nazis for an unspecified fate. Socialists and Communists were also arrested and held as political prisoners. Resentment at the occupation grew steadily.

Coastal defences surround the fuel storage tanks at Fagerstand in Norway. Although allocated a small German garrison, the Norwegians had an imposed government of Norwegian fascists led by Vidkun Quisling. An active resistance movement aided Britain by supplying information and assisting commando raids.

A member of the French Maquis resistance stands guard in central France. The first armed resistance grew in the countryside where men fleeing enlistment as slave labour or arrest gathered in groups. Many men were armed with old rifles hoarded from World War One or with weapons stolen from the Germans.

A British officer (left) camps with the French Resistance in Brittany, 1944. British secret services supplied resistance groups with arms and explosives and provided expert guidance on sabotage attacks and ambushes. By 1944 the French resistance had a national command structure and tens of thousands of activists.

Resistance heroine Marie France inspects the bath in the Gestapo torture rooms in Paris, November 1944. In their attempts to break the French resistance, the Gestapo, or secret police, resorted to routine torture of suspects and to creating an extensive network of informants. The regular army used more traditional methods, including the holding and execution of hostages.

German soldiers stand guard in Pilsudksi Square, Warsaw, 1939. From the start the German occupation of Poland was brutal. The population was registered according to race and nationality, The ethnic Germans, or those who claimed to be, received better rations and guaranteed jobs. Poles were treated with indifference. Jews and Gypsies were rounded up and forced to live in ghettos or sent to concentration camps.

German troops ladle out rations at a soup kitchen in Warsaw, October 1939. In the immediate aftermath of the German invasion Warsaw became crowded with refugees. Later 1.2 million Poles were expelled from the lands annexed by Germany, adding to the refugee problem.

A Polish family expelled from their home by the Germans in 1939. During the early days of German rule non-Germans suffered badly, as did any who had been active in politics or the civil service. In 1942 the strict racial rules were relaxed and those Poles who had lived in German Poland before 1918 were allowed to register as German.

Slave labourers, recruited from captured Polish soldiers, work at road repairs in Germany, 1940. The Germans turned to slave labour to man their war effort. Millions of men and women were taken to Germany to work in brutal conditions. Poland suffered worst of any nation. It is estimated that about 1-in-6 of the pre-war population lost their lives one way or another.

A bridal tram in Prague, probably in 1939. The Czech lands were occupied by the Germans in March 1939. At first conditions were relatively good as the Germans sought to make Bohemia a profitable and willing partner of the Greater Reich. Although there was no petrol for private vehicles, weddings and other celebrations were encouraged.

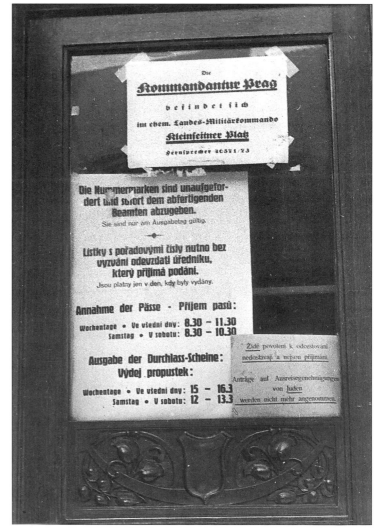

A notice at the Gestapo headquarters in Prague announcing regulations regarding travel permits. By 1942 conditions for Czechs had worsened as the war with Russia put a strain on German resources. The murder of German commander Reinhard Heydrich by the Czech resistance on 25 May 1942, led to a brutal reign of repression and massacre.

Lithuanian Nazis march through Memel. With recent and horrific experience of rule by both Tsarist and Soviet Russia, the Lithuanians welcomed the German invasion. Many Lithuanians volunteered to join the German forces fighting the Soviets. When the Soviets recaptured Lithuania, many thousands fled to escape the vengeance of the Soviet secret police, others began a guerrilla war which rumbled on until 1953.

Jews arrive at Auschwitz death camp, probably in 1944. Nazi racial hatred culminated in the systematic murder of Jews, Gypsies and others. It is unclear exactly how many died during the genocide launched by fanatical Nazis, but an estimate of around six million has been made.

Children peer from the barbed wire at Auschwitz as Allied troops arrive to liberate the camps. The network of camps included not just extermination gas chambers, but also slave labour camps, medical laboratories for experiments of repellent brutality and simple prison camps.

The liberation of Paris, 1944. A collaborator, beaten and stripped of his trousers is handed over to an American soldier by angry resistance fighters. The coming of liberation was often an excuse for old scores to be settled. Justice against collaborators was often brutal, swift and indiscriminate.

The Home Front

A policeman on duty outside the Houses of Parliament. The outbreak of war affected most aspects of everyday life for the people of Britain. Some changes were a mere inconvenience, others were more deadly. This policeman wears white sleeve guards so that his signals can be seen more easily during the black out and a metal helmet in case of sudden air raids.

NATIONAL REGISTRATION

IDENTITY CARD

UNDER SIXTEEN YEARS

Identity cards were introduced for all citizens and had to be carried at all times. Any policeman or other official could demand to see an identity card at any time. Introduced as a precaution against spies and deserters, the identity cards were not liked and there was much relief when they were abandoned after the war.

Mrs Witham of London tries to manage the ration books for her family. The careful use of ration coupons became a greatly admired skill among housewives with the wise use of coupons often making the difference between comfort and discomfort for a family.

A customer chooses a suit at Selfridges in May 1941. As with many other goods, a suit had both a money value and a coupon value. The number of coupons needed to purchase a product might vary as supplies increased or decreased.

Gas mask drill for the under-5s at a school in Windsor. Many young children from central London and other cities were evacuated to residential schools such as this where it was hoped that they would be safe from enemy bombing. Others remained at home and became accustomed to nightly visits to the air raid shelter.

A sympathetic glance from a grandmother to a baby waiting for its mother. The queue is for eggs available on strict ration from a shop in London which receives supplies direct from farms. Supplies were often erratic and dried eggs were introduced for use in cakes and pies. The yellow powder was considered unappetising and remained unpopular throughout the war.

Mothers and children made homeless by the Blitz in Bristol gather for dinner in a tent at a YWCA rest camp outside the city. Refugees were at first housed in such tented camps until more permanent accommodation could be found.

Mrs Wickard of Weston Turville hands over broken metal utensils to a group of schoolchildren collecting salvage in May 1943. The donation and collecting of scrap was considered a prime duty. Metal and rubber which could be recycled meant that fewer ships had to cross the U-boat infested Atlantic to bring raw materials to Britain.

As invasion threatened to become a reality in 1940 road signs were taken down across Britain. it was hoped that an absence of signs would confuse invading Germans or parachutists sent in to secure vital bridges. The removal of signs served only to confuse use the British with many travellers becoming hopelessly lost or getting off trains at the wrong station.

Railway porters given bayonet drill by a sergeant in the Guards, June 1940. Railway stations had been key targets for paratroops and advance troops during the German invasion of France, so British rail workers were key groups for military training in the Home Guard.

An elderly volunteer of the Home Guard parades with colleagues. Raised in 1940 from civilians exempt for military service, the Home Guard at first had few weapons Their tasks included guarding bridges, rail junctions and roads to free trained service personnel for combat duties.

In their early days the Home Guard was chronically short of equipment. Initiative and makeshift equipment was highly valued. This 'sniper' has a modern rifle, but has relied on local homemade camouflage to aid him in hiding among the bushes of Kent.

A section of mounted Home Guards leave for their night patrol, 1940 Patrolling the countryside in search of German paratroopers was one of the most important Home Guard duties. It was expected that any German invasion at dawn would be preceded by paratroop drops around midnight. Any paratroops caught would give valuable early warning of invasion. These men still wear arm bands marked LDV for Local Defence Volunteers, the original name of the Home Guard.

Men of the City of London Post Office Home Guard company take part in an exercise in 1941. By this time the Home Guard was equipped with uniforms and rifles. It was now expected to take a full role in street fighting to hold up German infantry in the event of an invasion.

A young couple leave Hyde Park to cross Park Lane in London, July 1942 The iron railings which had become such a feature of British towns and cities in Victorian times were removed across the country for melting down and use in armaments. Only those railings of special architectural value were left Many towns have never recovered from this sacrifice.

A British family tunes in to listen to a wireless broadcast. During the war years, the BBC became a much loved friend for many with its regular news broadcasts and light-hearted entertainment programmes The fact that this family have gas masks at the ready indicates the picture is an early one. After several months of German air raids without gas being used, most people neglected to carry their gas masks.

Polish airmen give a display of folk dancing together with WAAFs they have taught the female roles. After the Germans overran Europe refugees and fighting men from many nations found their way to Britain where they became a colourful feature of everyday life, though language problems caused difficulties at first.

Sid Fraser returns from the forces to his old place of employment at Hill Farm Turkey Farm, Norfolk. The raising of livestock by British farmers became vital to help increase the meat ration, especially at Christmas when a shortage of turkeys would have affected morale among civilians.

Land Army girls at work gathering in the grain harvest in Hertfordshire. With so many men away with the forces, women were recruited to work the land. This image of healthy outdoor work was far removed from the early starts, dirty lodgings and hard labour that many young women had to endure as they worked for victory.

Policemen of the Hyde Park Station Piggery proudly show off one of their porkers in 1941. Many work places had a pig club. Those who took turns at feeding, mucking out and generally caring for the pigs were rewarded with cuts of fresh meat whenever a pig was slaughtered.

Pekham policemen tend their Victory Garden in June 1940. The 'Dig for Victory' campaign urged everyone to convert gardens into allotments and grow their own fruit and vegetables so as to ease the burden on merchant ships bringing food into Britain from overseas.

Sergeant Penn of the Army Catering Corps proudly displays two pies, made to regulation recipes. With certain foods in desperately short supply, the government put much effort into formulating recipes from ingredients which could be more readiily obtained. Though useful in war time, such recipes were rarely popular and few survived the ending of rationing.

Perhaps the rarest food in Britain during wartime, bananas were counted a tropical luxury and disappeared from the shops. This man holds up two bunches, part of an 82-ton consignment which arrived with other goods on 5 February 1941. For most children their first taste of a banana did not come until 1946.

A policeman gives muffled instructions to a coach driver during gas mask drill in Brighton, February 1941. By this stage so few people regularly carried gas masks with them that a joke went around that German spies would be easy to spot as they would be the only ones thorough enough to remember a gas mask.

An exhausted William Hands comes off duty as part of an ARP Rescue Squad in November 1941. Given the task of digging through bombed buildings to try to locate survivors, ARP men worked long hours in exhausting and dangerous conditions. Most had daytime jobs as well, Mr Hands was a plumber.

A scene from the propaganda movie *The Urmpity Poo Girls,* part of a sales drive for War Savings Dividends. By investing in government bonds, ordinary people released their savings for the purchase of war materials while being assured of the return of their money, with interest, after the war. If Britain won that was.

A corner shop in Birmingham in 1940. Amid the familiar packets of food and other goods can be found posters for defence bonds, second hand clothing and the ration stamps which had become such a regular feature of shopping through the war years.

A woman puts up an election poster for the Cardiff by-election of April 1942. Although by-elections still took place to replace Members of Parliament who died, a national government had been formed by a coalition of parties. The national effort was directed at fighting the war and political activity largely came to an end.

US Sergeant Sullivan leaving the US Embassy in London with his new English wife after enquiring about arrangements to take his wife home in September 1945. The arrival of thousands of exotic American men in smart uniforms and with higher pay than British servicemen swept many women off their feet to become war brides, and caused some resentment among British servicemen.

A prefabricated house and garden is shown off in Croydon by a young couple in June 1945. Developed as an emergency measure to house the thousands made homeless by bombing, the 'prefab' as the houses were popularly called became a regular feature of British towns and villages. Some remained in use until the 1960s, although intended originally to last just ten years.

War at Sea

The SS *Kemmendine* is sunk by torpedo, 20 June 1941. The struggle to keep open the sea lanes was one that Britain could not afford to lose. Unable to produce enough food to feed her population, Britain would have been starved into surrender within a matter of weeks if Germany had cut off supplies.

The German pocket battleship *Admiral Graf Spee* photographed a few weeks before her final voyage. This powerful warship was at sea when war broke out and at once began sinking Allied merchant ships. A force of three British cruisers met and engaged the *Graf Spee* off the River Plate. The cruisers were badly damaged. The *Graf Spee* suffered minor damage and put into Montevideo for repairs. After being tricked into thinking a massive force of British ships was waiting offshore, the German commander scuttled his vessel.

A converted trawler drags a skid to set off magnetic mines. Magnetic mines proved to be a powerful weapon for the Germans, until the British learnt how to 'degauss' their ships and so reduce their magnetic signature. The skid was a device which emitted a large magnetic signal, setting off magnetic mines.

The wreck of the liner SS *Dunbar Castle*. Sunk by a mine in January 1940, the *Dunbar Castle* was carrying large numbers of civilians including women and children when she went down. The wreck was later destroyed with demolition charges as she was causing a hazard to navigation.

The last seconds of HMS *Glowworm* on 8 April 1940. On a reconnaissance mission covering British landings in Norway, the destroyer *Glowworm* encountered the German cruiser *Admiral Hipper* Although heavily outgunned, the *Glowworm* fought bravely, at one point ramming the larger ship. She was sunk minutes after this photograph was taken and the survivors captured. The incident has become an epic of the sea, but was unknown to the British until some months later.

The German battleship *Bismarck* opens fire on HMS *Hood*. The most powerful warship of her day, the *Bismarck* steamed into the Atlantic to prey on Allied merchant ships on 18 May 1941. On 24 May, *Bismarck* met the British ships HMS *Hood* and HMS *Prince of Wales*. In a short action the *Hood* blew up, and *Prince of Wales* was driven off. The Royal Navy ordered every available ship to steam for the North Atlantic and join the chase for the *Bismarck*.

Part of the crew of HMS *Dorsetshire,* a cruiser which helped sink the *Bismarck*. Having sunk the *Hood, Bismarck* headed into the Atlantic then turned for a French port for repairs.

Damaged by an air strike, the *Bismarck was* finally met by the battleships HMS *Rodney* and HMS *King George V* After a battle lasting over an hour, the German ship was sunk.

Minesweepers put to sea on 29 December 1941. The task of these armed trawlers was to clear coastal waters around Britain of mines laid by German ships and aircraft

Although rarely glamourous, their job was dangerous and vital to the war effort.

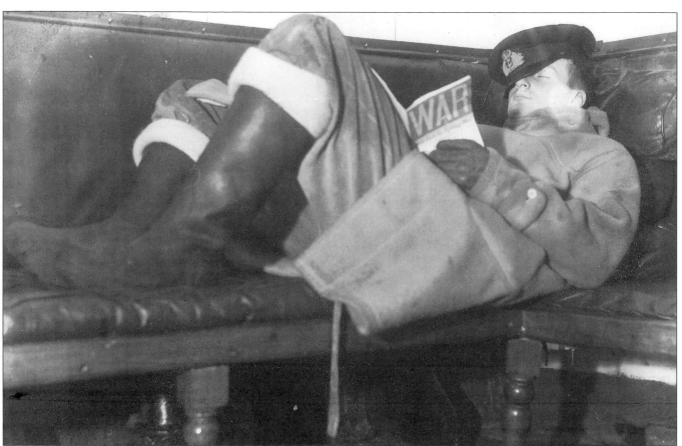

A lieutenant on a destroyer escorting a convoy in the North Atlantic snatches a few moments sleep. Convoy escort was a dangerous and demanding job as U-boats could launch attacks without warning, hurling the crews into instant action.

The destroyer HMS *Faulknor* steams past cruiser HMS *Sheffield* in 1940. On the outbreak of war destroyers had the task of guarding convoys of merchant ships or larger warships from torpedo attacks by submarines. Fast, manoeuvrable and generally under 2,000 tons, the destroyers were invaluable in the struggle against the U-boat as it developed in the North Atlantic.

A British trawler under attack by a German bomber, as seen from the attacking aircraft, 6 April 1940. The trawler was sunk. During the war, trawlers not only carried out their usual job of catching fish to help feed the population, but were also ideal for conversion to minelayers, mine-sweepers and various other auxiliary roles.

A U-boat commander at the controls of his craft. The U-boats proved to be the most effective anti-ship weapon of the Germans. During the war, German U-boats sank 2,828 merchant ships belonging to Allied nations and suffered 782 losses.

A German U-boat crew return to port during the early months of the war. Some U-boat commanders achieved celebrity status. Gunther Prien in *U47* entered the Royal Navy base at Scapa Flow and sank the battleship HMS *Royal Oak* just six weeks after war broke out. After sinking 28 other ships, he was killed when his submarine was destroyed on 8 March 1941.

A new U-boat leaves the naval yards of Krupp von Bohlen. By 1941 these works were the greatest naval building yards in the world, turning out naval guns and armoured steel as well as complete U-boats.

British survivors are photographed from a U-boat which took them prisoner on 1 December 1941. The war at sea rarely had time for such chivalry. Any U-boat which lingered on the surface too long risked being identified on radar and coming under attack from Allied aircraft or surface ships.

A German E-boat speeds through the North Sea. Built in large numbers these motor torpedo boats were used for raiding convoys in coastal waters and engaging minesweepers and other small naval craft. Although not as significant as the U-boats, the E-boats made a crucial impact in the North Sea and Mediterranean.

Battleships of the Italian navy open fire during a pre-war exercise off Naples. Although the Italian army had little success, the Italian fleet was highly regarded. After a series of largely inconclusive battles, the Italian navy pounced on a British convoy escorted by cruisers and destroyers in June 1942. The Italians almost wiped out the convoy. The Royal Navy effectively pulled out of the Mediterranean.

A British 'Dido' class destroyer in action against Italian aircraft in the Mediterranean. In October 1942 the British won the Battle of El Alamein and the Royal Navy returned to the Mediterranean in strength. By July 1943, the Royal Navy, joined by American ships, had secure enough control of the sea to escort an Allied invasion of Sicily.

German battlecruisers *Scharnhorst Gneisenau* and *Prinz Eugen* steam up the English Channel on 12 February 1942. The ships were based in Brest to launch forays into the Atlantic to attack convoys, sinking 22 ships in one day alone. The RAF inflicted damage by bombing, meaning the ships had to execute the famous Channel Dash to reach repair facilities at Kiel. The successful steaming by three large warships up the Channel was a severe embarrassment to the British.

A British 'V & W' class destroyer shepherds a merchant ship back into position in a convoy. Although equipped with sonar to locate U-boats, British destroyers faced defeat in the Battle of the Atlantic by the spring of 1943. Too few merchant ships were getting through to keep Britain fed and surrender was dangerously close.

A depth charge about to be fired from a 'Flower' class corvette. The decisive turn in the Battle of the Atlantic came in May 1943 when the Atlantic Gap was closed. This Gap was the stretch of ocean in which air cover could not be provided, allowing the U-boats to operate on the surface. After enough long-range aircraft had entered service, the U-boat menace receded.

Desert Rats

A British Valentine Tank surges through the sands of the North African desert, 1942. The war in North Africa began in 1940 with an Italian attempt to capture the Suez Canal and surge on to the oil fields of Iran beyond. Pushed back by the British and Imperial troops in Egypt, the Italians were reinforced by the Germans with Rommel and his legendary Afrika Korps. The war became one of swift movements and dramatic battles which ended with total Allied victory by 1943.

A company of the Egyptian Camel Corps patrols the open desert near Italian lines, 1940. Invaluable for patrolling the desert during pre-war days when the main problem was smuggling and Arab immigrants, the camels proved to be virtually useless in the face of Rommel's panzers and outflanking tactics.

A pipe band leads a regiment of South African Scots into Addis Ababa, April 1941. The first complete Allied victory in North Africa was the campaign to drive the Italians from Abyssinia, which they had occupied in 1936. Advancing from bases in Kenya and Sudan the British army was largely composed of Indian units and locally recruited regiments. The invasion began in January 1941 and took nearly 11 months of hard fighting until the last Italian garrison surrendered at Gondar in November.

Italian fighters fly in formation over the desert. Although equipped with aircraft which would be considered obsolete in Europe, the Italian air force in Libya was a force which had to be reckoned with by British commanders in Egypt. In the first months of war it totally dominated the skies over Egypt and launched many bombing raids on British positions.

An Arab guide shows a group of New Zealand troops, not yet issued with desert uniforms, the Pyramids and the Sphinx in February 1940. The ostensibly British 36,000-strong army in North Africa was actually drawn from many different parts of the British Empire. Australia, New Zealand, South Africa and India provided especially significant forces.

Grenade practice for New Zealand troops in Egypt. By July 1940 the New Zealand troops had been equipped with desert uniforms and were undergoing intensive training. Italy had declared war and British commanders expected an attack from the 250,000 Italian troops in Libya.

Italian anti-tank gunners dug in near Sollum. In September 1940 six Italian divisions marched into Egypt from Libya as the start of the invasions long promised by Mussolini. Italian commander, Rudolfo Grazianai, was not confident of success, however. He ordered his troops to dig in and lure the British on to concealed guns and tanks.

Italian prisoners being escorted to the rear by a British soldier after the battle at Beda Fomm, February 1941. The British attack from Egypt began on 7 December 1940, and achieved immediate success. Italian troops suffered from poor training, bad morale and inferior equipment. Rather than risk death in what they viewed as certain defeat, the Italians preferred to surrender.

Thousands of lead ingots piled up on a dockside, captured by the British in their advance into Libya. One of the main objectives of the Italian empire in North Africa was to acquire raw materials for the rapidly developing industries of Italy. The headlong British advance halted at El Agheila when the British ran out of supplies.

Australian troops in the streets of Trans-Jordan. The British mandated territory of Trans-Jordan served as a springboard for the invasion of Iraq in May 1941. Iraq had recently installed a pro-German government and threatened to disrupt the steady flow of vital oil to Britain. The campaign took just 29 days and cost under 70 casualties.

A warning sign erected by Australian infantry marks the front line in the desert. In March 1941 the British in North Africa realised they had come up against a much tougher adversary than the Italian army had proved to be. The German general Erwin Rommel, who had earned a formidable reputation for mobile warfare in the invasion of France, had arrived with the specially formed Afrika Korps, equipped with modern panzers and a massive amount of confidence.

A British 'cruiser' tank is inspected by a German after being knocked out. The photograph was taken by Rommel, a keen amateur photographer. The newly arrived Rommel quickly pushed the British out of Libya and back to Egypt, using his new panzers with tank-busting guns which outperformed anything the British had in the field. The British later equipped themselves with cruiser' tanks, a generic term which covered any type of tank designed for high speeds and armed with a cannon.

British tank crew tuck into standard rations near El Alamein, June 1942. The desert produced two features much hated by the men – sand and flies. Both managed to get into any food left uncovered for more than a few seconds and caused great discomfort and disease among the men at the front.

Below: British 25 pounder guns fire at night near El Alamein, 23 October 1942. After Rommel was stopped at El Alamein in July by General Auchinleck, the new British commander, Bernard Montgomery, launched his own attack in October. The attack opened with the 'greatest artillery bombardment of the desert war,' created by over 800 guns.

British infantry advance through shellfire, El Alamein. After 11 days of hard fighting and 10,000 casualties Montgomery's 8th Army broke through Rommel's positions and began to drive him westward out of Egypt. Rommel had lost 35,000 Germans and Italians as casualties or prisoners, together with most of his tanks.

Spahis, fighting for the Free French forces of General de Gaulle, set off an a mission behind enemy lines in the desert. A few days after the British victory at El Alamein massive American landings were made in French North Africa which threatened Rommel's supply routes. After at first fighting hard against the Americans, the local French commanders gave in and joined de Gaulle's forces.

A New Zealand Long Range Desert Group patrol enjoy a 'brew up' while scouting ahead of Montgomery's advancing army. Skilled at reconnaissance and sabotage, the LRDG played a small but significant role in the desert war. By 7 May, the Germans and Italians had been driven out of Africa completely.

Victory in the West

A Scottish soldier uses his bayonet to tear down a swastika flag in Cleves, Germany. After being driven from the continent in 1940, the British had to wait until 1944 until they could return to France. By that time the United States of America had joined the war and the Axis forces had been driven from North Africa.

Exhausted Canadian troops return from the raid on Dieppe in August 1942. The raid on Dieppe was designed to test theories for capturing a large port intact as a support base for a major invasion. The disastrous landings showed that such a step was impossible in the face of German resistance.

The personnel of an RAF bomber squadron poses with their Lancaster aircraft. After the failure of the Dieppe Raid the only way the Allies could strike at Germany was through bombing. The Lancaster could carry 14,000 lbs of bombs for 1,600 miles Suitable for long range raids, the Lancaster became the main aircraft used for bombing German cities at night, when defences were lighter.

A bumpy landing for an RAF Beaufighter in southern England. War flying was dangerous and risky. Enemy gunfire could not only kill crew and destroy aircraft, it could also damage sensitive controls in such a way that they did not break down until put under the stress of landings.

The crew of an American Flying Fortress bomber study the map of their route to Berlin, 1944. The Americans concentrated on daylight bombing to ensure greater accuracy using their new Norden bombsight. The decision led to greater damage to Germany's war industry, but also to horrific losses among American aircrew.

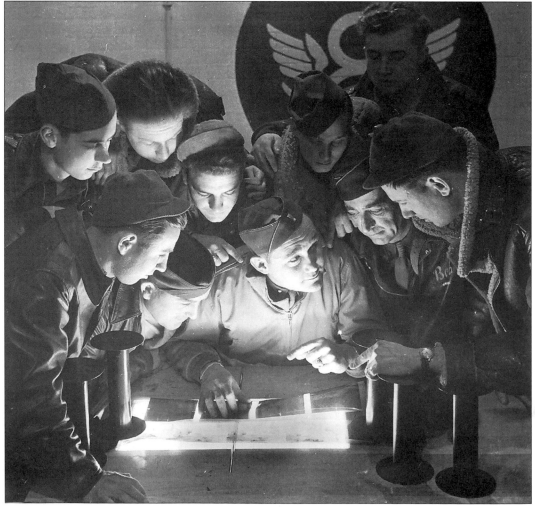

General Dwight Eisenhower talks to paratroops the day before they set off for France, 5 June 1944. The assault plan for D-Day called for paratroops to land at midnight and capture vital bridges and road junctions. They then had the task of holding their position until relieved by troops advancing from the beaches.

American troops load their equipment on to a landing craft ready for D-Day. Allied plans called for an assault wave made up of infantry supported by swimming tanks and preceded by a massive naval and aerial bombardment. Light armour such as on this craft would follow as soon as the beach was secured to help the push off the beach and move inland.

American troops find sparse shelter on Omaha Beach while landing craft bring up reinforcements early on D-Day. The Americans suffered dreadful casualties on Omaha after landing in the wrong place and encountering determined German resistance.

British and Canadian troops stream ashore on Juno Beach in the afternoon of D-Day. The Canadians enjoyed the greatest success on D-Day pushing seven miles inland before being struck by a counterattack by the 21 Panzer Division and forced on to the defensive.

The artificial Mulberry Harbour being put together at Arromanches-Les-Bains. The experience of Dieppe had taught Allied strategists that they would be unable to capture a port intact. Instead they constructed two artificial floating harbours capable of supporting the invasion for several weeks. The Mulberry harbours were in operation within ten days, but a storm later damaged one beyond repair.

American infantry march inland while landing craft ferry supplies and reinforcement to the beach from transport ships offshore. Although the Mulberry harbours handled the bulk of supplies, the demands of the fighting made it necessary to continue to import supplies over the sand for several weeks.

British Sherman tanks rumble through St Aubin-sur-Mer, captured late on D-Day. Having landed successfully, the main British objective was to push inland to Bayeux and Caen to secure a firm defensive line behind which

armour and other forces could be built up for a break out
attempt.

The ruins of Montebourg, one of several French villages destroyed as the Allies pushed inland from the D-Day beaches. The US VII Corps stormed through on 10 June on their way to Cherbourg, the nearest large port to the D-Day beaches. It was hoped to capture the port in working condition. However the German garrison held out long enough for demolition charges to put the port out of use for four months.

Troops of the American 7th Army enter Aix-en-Provence to liberate it from German occupation in August 1944. While the Allies were fighting a tough campaign across northern France, American and Free French forces landing near Nice in southern France encountered only weak opposition.

As Allied armies advanced across northern France a sudden crisis in Paris sparked a massed rising by the resistance and police forces. Following years of tradition in previous revolutions and rebellions, the French built barricades across the streets and prepared for an expected German counterattack.

Germans surrender to the resistance as Paris rises in rebellion, August 1944. Hitler had given General von Cholitz orders to demolish the main buildings of Paris and hold the rubble at all costs. Cholitz, however, had no intention of demolishing the city and had been stripped of too many troops to put up effective resistance for long.

Tanks of the Free French 2nd Armoured Division of General Phillipe Leclerc parked beside the Arc de Triomphe after fighting their way to Paris and accepting the German surrender on 25 August.

Parachutes and gliders litter the fields around Arnhem as the British 1 Airborne Division lands on 17 September. In a daring attempt to force the Rhine, Montgomery launched massive airborne landings to capture the bridges in Holland while an armoured thrust tried to break through to create a corridor along which the Allies could advance into Germany. The presence of two SS panzer divisions in Arnhem halted the advance and meant the Allies could not reach Germany before winter set in.

An American soldier looks down on the Remagen Bridge, March 1945. The Rhine was the last major natural obstacle facing the western Allies on their drive into Germany. On 7 March 1945, the US 9th Armoured Division discovered that the Remagen Bridge was still intact and raced across to capture it. Reinforcements were poured over to secure a bridge head.

The ruins of Cleves, March 1945. Cleves was one of the first German cities to be captured by the advancing western Allies. Fanatical resistance by the German garrison led to savage fighting and the near complete destruction of the city.

Infantry of the US Third Army rest in an alley in Geinsheim after crossing the Rhine The main Allied crossing of the Rhine, carried out along a 30-mile stretch of river and using 25 divisions took place around Wesel in late March. The Allies then paused to bring up massive reinforcement before beginning the final drive into Germany.

The US 1 Army marches into Germany. The open roads and lack of resistance once across the Rhine came as a surprise to the Allies. Although some Nazis held out with fanatical bravery, many senior German commanders realised that Germany was defeated. They wanted the western Allies to advance as swiftly as possible and occupy most of Germany before the Soviets arrived.

American Shermans move forward into Germany, Although inferior to the opposing German armour, the Shermans were available in vast numbers and were easy to service and handle in combat. Their main drawback was the thin armour over the engine, which meant a direct hit almost invariably led to a fire which destroyed the tank.

Corporal J.H. McConville of Ontario enjoys a bath in a forest in Germany. The pounding by bombers and artillery which preceded the Allied advance wrecked many houses, leaving household good strewn across the countryside. The advancing troops were only too happy to make use of whatever remained intact.

Germans surrender to the Americans near Gambsheim. As the German army collapsed the various units hurried westward to surrender to the Americans or British. Not only would the western Allies be less likely to take bloody and indiscriminate revenge than were the Soviets, but the wealthy Americans could be relied upon not to steal German watches and other personal belongings.

The empty shell of Berchtesgaden It was at this favourite residence that Hitler had laid the final plans of the invasion of the Soviet Union and from where he responded to the growing Allied advance in Normandy three years later. By May 1945 it lay in ruins.

A dazed German man sits on the ruins of his home after the British advance in northern Germany swept past him. On 30 April, Hitler committed suicide and on 2 May the few remaining defenders surrendered to the Soviets. On 4 May, German forces in western Germany surrendered to Montgomery in front of the news cameras and three days later a formal document was signed under which all forces surrendered to Eisenhower. The war in Europe was over.

A German refugee hauls her few remaining household possessions past British troops outside Cleves as Germany rushed towards total collapse. By mid-April the advancing American forces had met Soviet troops on the Elbe and Berlin had been surrounded. German forces began surrendering wholesale on various fronts. Only in Berlin did fanatical resistance by dedicated Nazis continue.

Defeat of Japan

An American correspondent views the wreckage of Hiroshima a few days after the atomic bomb was dropped. The defeat of Japan was brought about only by a long and costly campaign which began almost as soon as the Japanese tide of conquest reached its greatest extent in the late summer 1942. Even when victory seemed assured, the fanatical courage and utter ruthlessness of the Japanese military seemed to promise that the final battle would be extremely costly. Then America dropped its atomic bombs.

Private Lavell of Newport, Monmouthshire, advances cautiously past the temple at Bahe, Burma. The Chindit operations of 1943 and 1944 probed deep behind Japanese lines, but it was not until January 1945 that the British were able to advance. Armed with air superiority, better weapons and, most important, using new jungle tactics, the British surged over the Chindwin River into Burma proper.

Indian machine gunners in the battle for Fort Dufferin, Mandalay, The capture of Mandalay by General Slim's army on 20 March proved to be a turning point in the Burma campaign. The Japanese forces were effectively cut in two and were forced to abandon most of their heavy equipment in their retreat to the Shan Hills.

British Lee tanks manoeuvre under fire to assault Japanese positions at Ywathitgyi, Burma. On 1 May, Operation Dracula was launched to capture Rangoon, capital of Burma. The advancing British troops met heavy resistance, but by 6 May, the Japanese had abandoned the city. Burma was almost liberated.

A column of Australian supply trucks negotiates a road in New Guinea. Strategically important for the defence of both Australia and the East Indies, New Guinea was coveted by both Japan and the Allies. A Japanese landing at Buna in July 1942 failed to take Port Moresby, but led to years of savage fighting in the inhospitable jungles.

Clarrie Martin, a cabinet minister from New South Wales, inspects the traditional weapons of New Guinea tribesmen. In 1942 the fighting spilled over across the remote and densely forested inland mountains of New Guinea. Many tribes had never heard of either white men or Japanese before the fighting ranged across their territory.

Corporal Bill Horner of Australia supervises bean planting at Madang, New Guinea. In an attempt to win over the native tribes and to ease a chronic supply problem, the Allies introduced New Guinea tribesmen to crops such as tomatoes, paw paws and mangoes which grew prolifically and produced more food than the traditional local crops.

Local tribesmen carry wounded Australian troops to safety along the Kokoda Trail, New Guinea. The Kokoda Trail saw perhaps the most savage fighting in New Guinea's three years of war. In places less than a yard wide, the track was the main route over the Owen Stanley Mountains and passed through dense jungle and precipitous mountains. Allied supply problems were only solved when an airstrip was hacked out of the jungle.

Fascinated troops watch as Captain Gray gives emergency dental care to Private Verity near Mubo, New Guinea. The Australian forces which fought through New Guinea became accustomed to poor food and appalling fighting conditions. The visits of medical teams, such as this, not only eased nagging pains, but provided great entertainment for the patient's comrades.

Australian troops gratefully suck ice blocks captured from Japanese supply stores at Lae, New Guinea. The main Japanese base at Buna was captured in January 1943, but isolated pockets of resistance held out for another two years. Australians lost nearly 6,000 men to the Japanese, and twice as many to the jungle and its diseases.

Filipino President Osmena reads a speech while US General Douglas MacArthur (in sunglasses) awaits his turn at the microphone, Taclogsan, Philippines. The US invasion of the Philippines began on 20 October 1944, as troops landed on Leyte. The attack was a personal vindication for MacArthur who had been forced to leave three years earlier, uttering the immortal words "I shall return". His first words into the microphone at Taclogsan were, "I have returned".

A Japanese cruiser of the Mysho class turns desperately to avoid US bombs. The American landings in the Philippines provoked a massive Japanese response. Four Japanese fleets containing 64 ships converged on Leyte to tackle the invaders. The Americans concentrated 218 ships of various kinds in what became the the Battle of Leyte Gulf, the greatest naval battle of all time.

The Japanese battleship, *Yamato,* the most powerful battleship ever to be built. The *Yamato* led the main Japanese strike force at the Battle of Leyte Gulf. although skilful manoeuvring almost gave the Japanese victory, lack of air cover at the crucial moment led to their near complete destruction. The Japanese navy was never again a real threat.

US infantry enter San Fabian on Luzon, Philippines, March 1945 The American advance through the Philippines was slow and painful. The capture of Manila led to desperate fighting in which the city was utterly destroyed.

A Japanese kamikaze aircraft plunges toward the USS *Hornet* With their fleet out of action, the Japanese turned to desperate measures. Kamikazes were often ordinary aircraft loaded with explosives, but later a specific type of piloted bomb was designed for these suicide missions.

A young Japanese pilot, photographed with samurai sword before setting off on a kamikaze mission. The first onslaught of suicide attacks caught the Allies entirely by surprise and inflicted massive damage. At one point the Americans considered calling off all operations in the Philippines. But as Allied ship captains became better at evading the kamikaze attacks casualties fell.

A Hellcat fighter explodes as it crash lands on the USS *Lexington*. Faced with the task of capturing a large number of Japanese-held islands spread across thousands of miles of ocean, the American Pacific fleet developed sophistic-ated assault tactics. These began with air strikes launched from air craft carriers lying out of sight of the islands.

American cruisers open fire at an unspecified Pacific island. Following the air strikes came naval barrages to hit bunkers and strongpoints located by aerial reconnais-sance. The bombardment could go on for days against particularly strongly defended islands.

Amphibious Amtracs head for the beach at Iwo Jima. Following the naval bombardment the US Marines were sent ashore in armoured amphibious vehicles. Their task was to take and secure a section of beach from which the invasion could develop.

Landing craft (tank) vessels unload their cargo onto the beach at Nosmfeer Island. Once the infantry had secured a beachhead, larger landing craft brought up tanks and other armoured vehicles to lead the push inland to capture the bunkers and concealed emplacements at the positioning and holding of which the Japanese were so skilled.

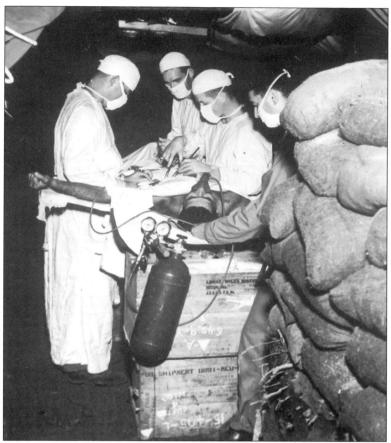

A makeshift medical centre on Bougainville Island. As soon as the heavier fighting equipment was ashore, temporary medical and tactical control centres were established. A pit was dug and lined with sandbags while heavy logs protected it from shrapnel from above. Such temporary structures could be built in a few hours and served until the fighting moved on out of small arms range.

US Marines seek shelter amid the desolate landscape of Tarawa, November 1943. Tarawa was one of the first islands to be assaulted by the Americans in their advance across the Pacific. The Marines lost over 1,000 dead in just three days due to poor co-ordination between the naval and marine forces. Valuable lessons were learnt which were put into practice later.

US Marines benefit from emergency first aid on Tarawa on Day Two of the invasion. Each Marine was expected to care for such minor wounds as this in the front line. The coconut logs covered with sand and packed with leaves seen behind these men was typical of the structure of Japanese bunkers on Pacific islands.

A US Marine sleeps exhausted during the assault on Peleliu Island, October 1944. The concentrated nature of the fighting on Pacific islands during the first stages of an assault meant that men might be under fire for up to two days without respite. Soldiers tended to fall asleep where they lay as soon as relieved by reinforcements.

US Marines land supplies on the beach on Peleliu. The casual attitudes of the men show this was after the island was declared secure. By late 1944 the Japanese had learnt to hide small detachments as the American assault rolled inland. The Japanese would burst from cover some hours later to mow down unsuspecting supply forces. The Americans became very apprehensive in rear areas during island assaults.

US Marines huddle for cover in the black sand of Iwo Jima just minutes after landing, 19 February 1945. Iwo Jima proved to be perhaps the toughest island the Americans had to assault. The deep black sand made the going impossible for most vehicles, while the infantry found themselves pinned down by skilfully sited artillery and machine guns.

An aerial view of Hiroshima after the dropping of the atomic bomb, 6 August, 1945. The appalling casualties suffered by the US forces attacking the island of Okinawa in April had convinced President Truman that the Japanese would fight to the bitter end leading to massive Allied casualties and the virtual extermination of Japan. He therefore authorised the dropping of the atomic bombs on Hiroshima and Nagasaki. Over 150,000 people died. Japan surrendered a few days later, averting the need for a traditional assault on the Japanese islands.

An American Coast Guardsman tends the graves of US Marines on the Philippines in the first days of peace. The campaign to defeat the Japanese had been costly to all involved, but the highest casualties were those suffered by Japan as American bombers flattened cities and Allied troops smashed armies.

The V-Days

Searchlights bathe St Paul's Cathedral in light as peace returns to the world. World War Two was the most costly in human history, with casualties totalling well over 40 million worldwide and material damage beyond counting. The ending of the fighting led to a great outpouring of emotion, first as spontaneous celebrations engulfed the streets and then in the more sober official parades and celebrations.

General Courtney Hodges of the US 1st Army and General Zhadov of the Soviet 5th Army toast each other during a joint reception at Torgau-am-Elbe in Germany on 4 May 1945. The meeting of the American and Soviet armies in Germany marked the end of the German army as an organised force, although sporadic resistance continued for some days.

Workmen prepare the lights of Fleet Street for a return to peacetime standard street lighting after years of the blackout, 5 May 1945. The return of everyday luxuries such as this had the greatest immediate effect on Britain following the surrender of Germany.

Crowds surge through Trafalgar Square. The news of Germany's official surrender on 8 May brought the crowds out on to the streets of London.

A group of young women outside Buckingham Palace on 8 May. The Royal Family had served as a focus for British resistance during the war, and Buckingham Palace became the spontaneous centre for the street celebrations when the war ended.

A mixed group of servicemen from different countries and civilians celebrate peace in Europe as the revels continue late into the night.

A couple embrace in a London pub as the news of Germany's final surrender reaches London.

A young woman celebrates on the afternoon of 8 May in Piccadilly as crowds mill around the boarded-up Eros statue behind her.

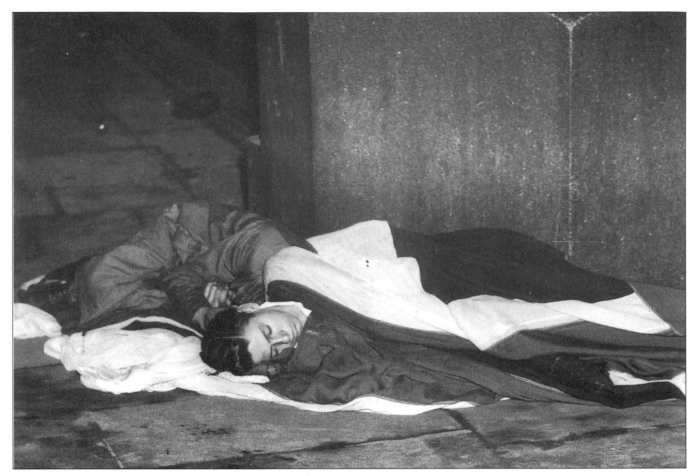

Taken at 3.30am on the night after VE Day, this photo shows two of the many who had to sleep on the streets of London after missing the last public transport home.

Still celebrating three days after VE Day, this child has a pram draped in a Union Jack while its mother goes shopping in London.

Children enjoy a street party at Sutton Dwellings in Chelsea a few days after VE Day itself. As the news sank in people had time to organise proper parties and to look forward to the return of their loved ones.

A policeman carries a lost child through the crowds which poured into the streets of London after the news was announced that Japan had surrendered. The outpouring of relief on VJ Day was, if anything greater than on VE Day, The fighting was finally over and the sudden nature of the collapse of Japan made the peace all the more surprising.

VJ Day crowds in The Mall, looking towards Admiralty Arch. As on VE Day, Buckingham Palace served as a centre for the crowd's spontaneous celebrations.

The Victoria Monument outside Buckingham Palace provides a grandstand view of the celebrations taking place in the warm August sunshine.

A young woman wears a newspaper, the headline of which says it all, in London's West End on VJ Day.

Crowds block the route of buses through Piccadilly on VJ Day.

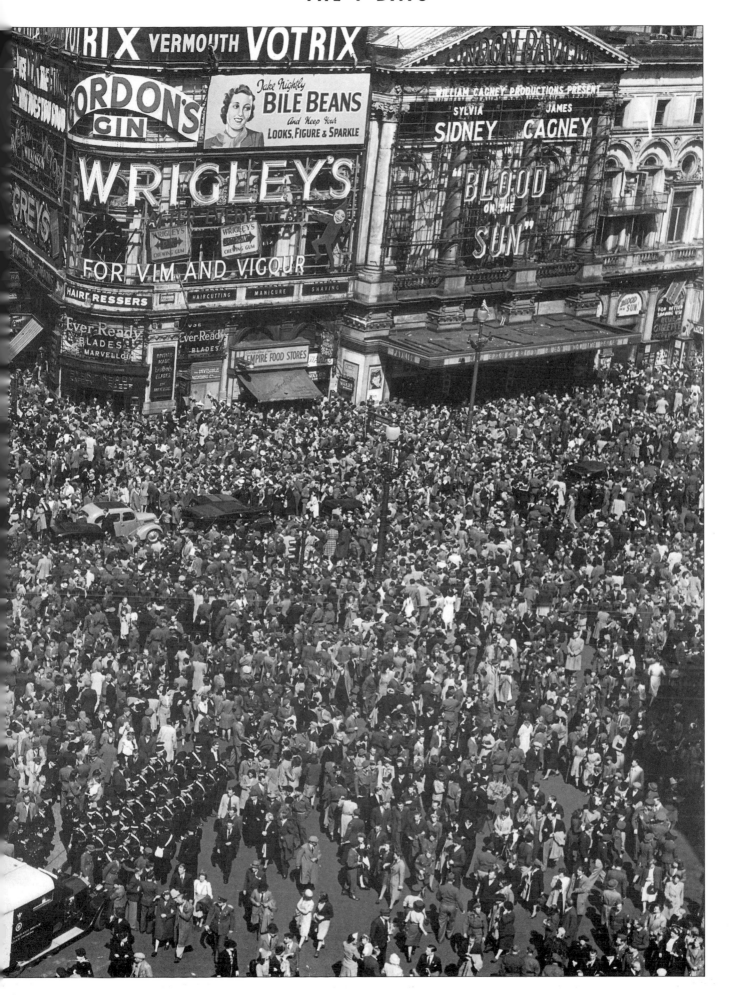

A child enjoys dessert during a VJ street party in Lowell Street, Limehouse, on 7 August. As with VE Day, the street parties continued for some days after the news broke as people got themselves organised.

VJ Dancers in Regent Street in London's West End. Many of the main thoroughfares were effectively closed to traffic as the crowds took over the streets.

A young woman is tossed high into the air by joyful crowds as VJ Day celebrations move into the evening.

An impromptu bonfire burns in Piccadilly as the crowds continue to celebrate late into the night.

Council workmen from the City of London move in to clear up the streets after VJ Day.

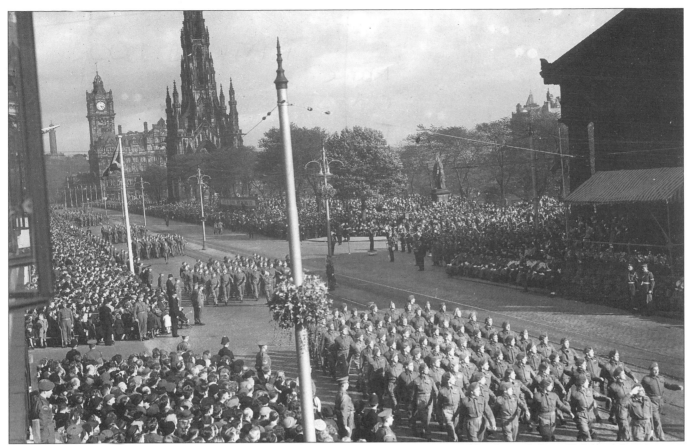

The Edinburgh Victory Parade in September 1945. The Edinburgh parade was the first of the official celebrations to be organised after the close of hostilities.

Dock workers throw newspapers to returning prisoners of war, eager for news of home. The arrival of PoWs from the Far East showed the public for the first time that the horrific stories they had been hearing of Japanese treatment of prisoners were all too true.

Canadians lead the Empire Detachments in the great Victory Parade through London on 8 June 1946. A total of 21,000 troops and 480 vehicles marched through the streets to pay tribute to the many millions who had served both at the front and at home.

Corporal Percy Toms of Ewell, Surrey, leads the released PoWs on to British soil as the first ship of Japanese PoWs arrives in Britain. The ceremonial welcome given to the returning prisoners, did little to ease the bitterness they felt towards the Japanese. It was a bitterness which they harboured for many years.

Four London Buses parade through Admiralty Arch. The civilians were not forgotten during the Victory Parade of 1946. The familiar red buses had continued running even in the worst days of the Blitz, keeping London on the move and able to work.

New World Order

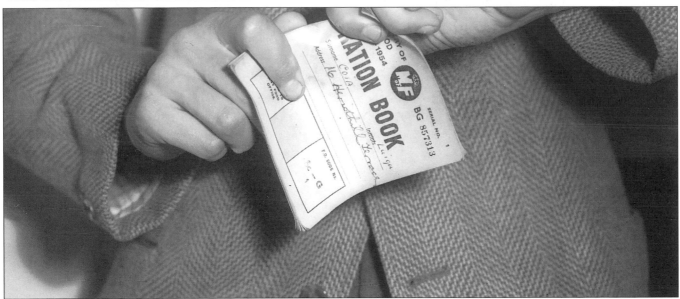

A man tears up his ration book in October 1953. The return of peace brought many changes to the world, Soviet power extended enormously and the United States took a more active foreign policy role. However, peace did not mean the immediate end to wartime restrictions and shortages, as people in many countries were to learn.

British military policemen stop a German civilian to check his identity papers in Bielefeld, 1947. as an army of occupation the Allies had the task of removing the vestiges of Nazism from Germany while establishing a civilian government and rebuilding the housing and industries of the shattered nation.

A view of the Bochum steel works, only three chimneys show signs of life, while nearby land has been given over to growing grain. The scene was typical of post-war Germany, The once great industries were reduced to a fraction of their pre-war size while land was hurriedly converted to growing food to feed the homeless and largely distressed population.

A general view of the courtroom during the Belsen Trial, one of the Nuremburg War Crimes Trials. Those accused of crimes sit to the left with numbers on their chests.

Belsen was the first of the concentration camps to be captured by the advancing Allies, on 13 April 1945 The horrors it contained greatly shocked the public.

The accused at the main Nuremburg Trial. Goering is in the pale suit and wears dark glasses while Rudolf Hess sits next to him. The main charges included conspiracy to wage a war of aggression, breaking the rules of war and crimes against humanity, such as the mass murder of Jews and others.

Journalists rush from Nuremburg Trial after the verdicts were announced on 1 October 1946. Three Nazis were acquitted, and eleven were sentenced to death. Hess was sentenced to life in prison, dying in 1987. Goering was sentenced to death, but committed suicide before the sentence could be carried out. The Gestapo and SS were declared to be criminal organisations.

Three British troops resist the attempts of a German woman to fraternise, Hamburg. Fraternisation, or 'fratting', was strictly banned for the army of occupation. Officers feared assassination attempts by die-hard Nazis and that their men would be slack in their duty if they became too friendly with the locals. As the army of occupation became an established feature of German life, the ban on fratting was gradually eased.

A busy telephone room at the Ministry of Fuel and Power at the height of the 1947 fuel crisis. The fuel shortage struck Britain as the growing demands of industry and the domestic market outstripped the ability of the coal mines to keep up production increases. The reaction of the newly installed Labour government was to establish a Ministry of Fuel and Power. Civil servants became involved in the business of producing fuel and rationing it out between competing demands.

The men of the Parc and Dare Colliery in Treorchy who raised 2,300 tons of coal on their first working Sunday, 7 February 1947. The fuel crisis forced the government to take drastic steps to boost output, including asking Welshmen to work on the sabbath.

Volunteers gather a petition asking Dwight Eisenhower, the successful American general of the European war, to stand for President in the 1948 elections. Eisenhower refused, but he stood in 1952 after retiring from the army, His two terms in office saw an attempt to move closer to China, but also saw the sudden and dramatic collapse in relationship with the Soviet Union.

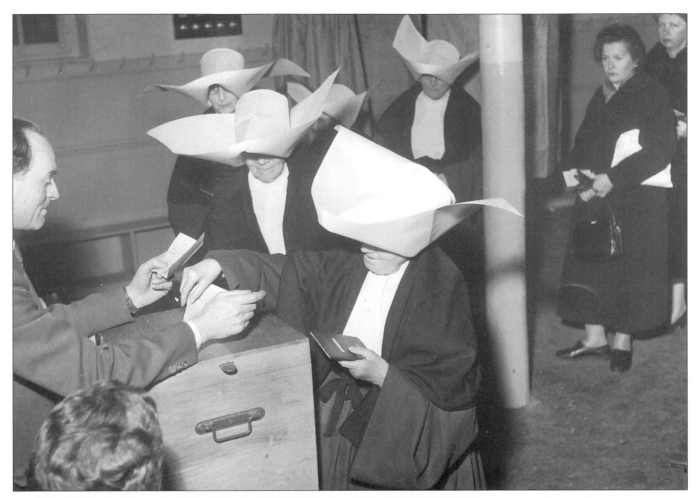

Nuns take their turn voting in the first French elections to be held after the war. The election followed two years in which General Charles de Gaulle, who had led the Free French forces, served as provisional President while a new Constitution was drawn up for what became the 4th Republic. After some years in quiet retirement, de Gaulle returned to politics in 1958, taking control of the nation at the height of the Algerian crisis.

A public meeting in Kashmir debates the future of the kingdom. In 1947 Britain pulled out of the Indian sub-continent after creating two successor states, Hindu India and Moslem Pakistan. Kashmir lay on the border between the two and had a religiously divided population. The Maharajah of Kashmir decided to join India, which led to fighting and bitterness which has not yet faded.

Rioting in Bombay, 1948. The division of India into two new countries, based on religion led to much unrest. The Indian government was particularly keen to stamp out dissent and unrest. The rioting in Bombay followed the decision to ban a meeting of students which was expected to be highly critical of the government.

A portrait of Stalin dominates a shop window, Prague, 1948. After being liberated by the Soviets in 1945 Czechoslovakia was formed from the minor states created by the Nazis. The pre-war government was reinstalled in power, though Stalin insisted that the Communist resistance be given a place in government. In 1948 the Soviets inspired a coup which led to the country becoming a Communist dictatorship and Soviet satellite.

Citizens of Berlin wave a welcome to an incoming cargo aircraft during the Berlin Air Lift. In February 1948 talks between the four occupying powers broke down over the future of Germany, The following month the Soviets imposed a block on all road and rail transport to the western Allies' zones of Berlin, deep in the Soviet area of Germany in an attempt to gain control of the entire city.

A Soviet military policemen halts a British truck to check papers as the first road convoy reaches Berlin, May 1949. For over a year a continual stream of Allied cargo aircraft carried food, clothes and fuel into Berlin, daring the Soviets to take action to stop them. Eventually Stalin had to accept he could not take Berlin by starvation. The roads were reopened and Germany became divided into two countries, one democratic and one Communist.

A truck load of Communist supporters drive through the almost deserted streets of Berlin to encourage citizens to vote for the approved list of Communist candidates. Despite the fact that only Communists were allowed to stand by the Soviets, the elections of May 1949 proved to be a deep embarrassment. Few people turned out to vote, and many of those who did deliberately spoilt their papers to show disapproval. Soviet might nevertheless imposed a Communist government.

Diplomats meet in London to inaugurate the North Atlantic Treaty Organisation, or NATO, as it became better known, 1951. Growing out of the 1949 North Atlantic Treaty which banded 20 democratic nations together to oppose Soviet expansion, the organisation became the foremost military organisation of the free world during the Cold War.

Mrs Carrington-Ward organises a petition in May 1950 to demand the resignation of John Strachey, War Minister, and Emanuel Shinwell, Defence Minister, because of alleged Communist links. As the power of the Soviet Union grew and became more openly hostile to the West, many people began to fear a repeat of the appeasement which had proved to be so fatal against Hitler. A firm line against Communism was demanded from politicians.

The 'Red Dean' Dr Hewlett Johnson, Dean of Canterbury, leaves a stormy meeting in St Pancras, July 1952. In 1950, the democratic South Korea and Communist North Korea went to war, with the opposing super powers taking sides and sending in troops. Dean Johnson provoked uproar by visiting China and coming back with what he claimed was evidence that American troops were using poison gas.

The men of the 'Japanese People's Emancipation League', a unit of Japanese based in Communist China and dedicated to taking over Japan. The establishment of Communist control in China in 1949 after a civil war was of concern to the western nations. When China began interfering in neighbouring states and backing Communist parties throughout Asia that worry became even greater.

A sick woman is carried to vote at elections in Austria, February 1953. Like Germany, Austria had been divided into zones of occupation by the Allied powers. After the Berlin airlift and subsequent division of Germany, many Austrians feared their nation would go the same way, The elections were considered to be extremely important, and their success led to Austrian independence as a single nation in 1955.

Soviet tanks guard the town hall of Gyoer, Hungary, in November 1956. Stalin imposed a Soviet style government on Hungary in 1945, but his death in 1953 led to popular unrest and some measures of freedom were instigated by Prime Minister Imre Nagy. After a period out of office, Nagy returned to power in 1956, declaring Hungary a neutral state and appealing to the United Nations for protection. On 4 November that year, under orders from Stalin's successor, Nikita Kruschev, the Soviets invaded, brushing aside unco-ordinated resistance and demonstrations. Nagy and others were murdered and 190,000 fled into exile.